Philippe Gilbert

Philippe Gilbert

My year in top gear

LANNOO

Table of contents

PREFACE

I admit it without shame: I have more than once been jealous of the glories of the journalists of the Sixties and Seventies who had the privilege of living with the wheels of Eddy Merckx. Like the immense Luc Varenne, who allowed himself to inform the 'Cannibal', from his motor bike, on the gaps during the race.

Huge ! Merckx brought sunshine into my childhood by a relationship that was close to fanaticism, and he also inevitably led me towards other heroes of the pen or the microphone, heralds of the verb and of superlatives. So it was not by chance that, one day, I myself became a witness of the cycle race, imprisoned between passion and the conscious duty of benefiting from an absolute privilege. Despite everything, I still was jealous of my elders while I fretted from boredom in races that were devoid of relief, panache, star or suspense. My 'Merckxitude' remained rooted in my memory and I have sometimes great difficulty in enchanting the verb to bring to my readers the testimony of events that are excruciatingly banal. The shattering disclosure of the doping affairs did not help to exteriorise my enthusiasm. On the contrary, it set itself up as a weighty battering ram to break the wall that my naivety had constructed. It was salutary for establishing a more objective relationship with cycling and especially for saving the latter from an announced death. May the players of the Festina affair therefore be publicly thanked here: they have provoked an indispensable humanitarian action for their successors.

Philippe Gilbert had just celebrated his sixteenth birthday when Richard Virenque cried in front of millions of television viewers. The kid from Remouchamps was overwhelmed by it and reckoned, on that particular day, that his passion would require the most elementary prudence. It was this conscious, lucid, serene young man, devilishly absorbed by his objectives, whom I met for the first time on the other side of the Atlantic, at the world championships of Hamilton (Canada) where the Belgian team brought back a medal via Peter Van Petegem. Since that meeting, I'm no longer jealous of my French masters, Blondin or Chany. I regret on the contrary that they could not cross the path of Philippe Gilbert, the sportsman who, no matter what occurs, will have marked my career, and not only by his results. The man and the champion have almost succeeded in moderating my 'Merckxitude', but isn't this normal as of the moment when Gilbert will finish by becoming the greatest Belgian champion since the Cannibal? I had, furthermore, in this year of 2011, nicknamed him the 'little Cannibal'. It is to thank him for having brilliantly rekindled the fire of my passion for the most beautiful of sports that I will readily be his guide in the writing of this book, that of an historical 2011 season that was unable to await the end of a career before being recounted for ever and a day.

Stéphane Thirion

CHAPTER 1
A Dream Season's Origins

I'm astonished when people are astonished, either admiringly or distrust-ingly, by Philippe Gilbert's superlative season. As if his successes had arrived like Martians landing from who knows where! It's simply enough to go back in time a little to measure the linearity of the Remouchamps champion. To note that places of honour have mutated towards the highest step, that work, age and maturity have evolved in perfect parallel with the wheels of Philippe's bicycle. I was struck by his comment on the evening of the Liege-Bastogne-Liege won by Valverde. '*It's the most beautiful but I don't know if I can win it: it's perhaps too hard for me. I perhaps have a better chance of winning the Tour of Flanders.*' However, Phil still hasn't won the Round but indeed the Doyenne (the Oldest). And it was certainly in Lombardy that he paved the way for his future coronation in the Ardennes. In 2009, a few weeks after having served as a springboard for his Lotto teammate, Cadel Evans, on the very demanding Mendrisio World Championships course, Gilbert relied on the rainbow jersey to treat himself to his first 'monu-ment', the Tour of Lombardy, after beating the Olympic champion, Samuel Sanchez. To warm up, he had already scorched the roads of Piedmont a few days earlier. And to forget nothing about that particular autumn, he had also treated himself to the luxury of a double on the Avenue de Grammont in Tours by deposing none other than his compatriot, Tom Boonen. On that evening, I had had the privilege of sharing his table and, before we left, he declared: '*You can make the trip to Lombardy: you won't be disappointed.*'

It was the first time that he spoke to me like that with such self- assurance at the approach of an objective. And what an objective! Because, finally, Phil hadn't yet met with success in the Amstel, the Arrow, or the Liege. Many ended up confining him to a more 'Flemish' role, much more effective in San Remo or Meerbeke than on the slopes of the Madonna del Ghisallo. And yet. Something was triggered on the banks of Lake Como. And that did not escape the Italians, very mindful of the quality and the panache of champions, whatever their nationality. Gilbert's moult concretely occurred in October 2009. It was confirmed by a brilliant success in the Amstel Gold Race 2010. The well-known, now famous, 'spurt' of the man from Remouchamps, in particular in the Tour of Spain where, twice, he resisted the pack by clenching his teeth to set himself up as the number one favourite for the Geelong World Championships in Australia, where a damnable headwind interrupted the excessiveness of his extraordinary effort.

On that particular day, I feared that I might discover a shattered man, beyond the line where the Norwegian national anthem resounded to the skies to the glory of Thor Hushovd. He expressed no regret however, and although the night was difficult, the next day he was inquiring about what was needed for the journey to Italy for the defence of his titles in the Piedmont and in the Lombardy. Which other cyclist, in the current peloton, could take such immediate stock, and immediately refocus on another objective?

In Como, in any case, the Geelong sun was only a distant memory. The autumn had already largely taken hold of the banks of the lake where the trees, hastily deprived of their foliage, were taking advantage of the mist to make themselves scarves from it. It was raining cats and dogs, and morale was needed to hoist ones shorts for the Ghisallo ascent where the Madonna was shivering on her headland. After having benefitted from his team mates' colossal work, Gilbert also showed that he was an excellent downhiller, spurning the runnels of rain and the pebbles disgorged by the saturated verges. By some superb feat of gymnastics, at 50 kilometres from the arrival, he caused the fall of his most dangerous rival, Vincenzo Nibali, unable to follow the tightrope walker from the Ardennes. The weather, frightful, had disrupted all communication by earpiece. When Roberto Damiani, his Sports Manager, finally managed to catch up with him, Gilbert asked him about the race situation because the earpiece wasn't working. The Italian revealed to him that Scarponi was between the breakaway group and the pack, and that he wasn't tiring. This short conversation was sufficient to transform the interior of the Omega Pharma-Lotto car into a sauna. And Gilbert waited for Scarponi, whom he could very well have had at the sprint. But he wanted to arrive on his own, to benefit from this transitory but succulent pleasure of preparing his appearance in the light from the flashes with effect from the 500-metre panel. He attacked Scarponi on the final rise of San Fermo della Battaglia where Scarponi pretended to have a derailleur problem in order to avoid admitting humiliation from his adversary.

Escorted by the headlights of the race management car, Gilbert crossed the Como line in torrential rain. His jacket was so soaked that it made him a second skin. The television reporters huddled together in a tent that was threatening to collapse under the weight of the water. One could read the admiration in the onlookers' eyes because, quite clearly, in the country of Coppi and other exceptional cycling wizards, Philippe Gilbert had just achieved the feat of his career. It was premonitory. The *Gazzetta dello Sport* christened him, on the day after the sacred Lombardy, the 'King of the Classics'. The pink newspaper didn't realise how right it was.

From the arrival to the press room, a frail barque brought him by the lake to save time because, that very evening, the Flemish public television channel, VRT, was expecting him for a live broadcast in order to present him with the Fleming of the Year Trophy. The first of a long list of awards, and therefore of the social obligations that Philippe dislikes.

'The champagne offered by Thor Hushovd'

The after-race proceedings, in Lombardy, were a genuine stopwatch event: the podium, the TV and radio press, the anti-doping control and the press conference, but with the victory, all that is less of a burden and then it was the end of the season. Afterwards, I returned to the team bus, where Thor Hushovd and Olivier Kaisen among others were waiting for me. We drove to Lugano where a private plane was waiting for us. I had a shower in the bus while it was on the move, and then I got into my suit. Direction Brussels and to the VRT set in order to receive the Fleming Trophy to which the organizers had invited Thor for his rainbow jersey. A police escort threaded its way from Zaventem to Reyers without observing the speed limits: it was exhilarating. There, I suddenly felt important but it only lasted a couple of hours, which was probably just as well. Hushovd had bought a magnum of Champagne which had cost him an arm and a leg in a little bar in Lugano. A few of us drank it together before entering the wings of the VRT programme, which had already started! Then, I went to have a drink in town with Jürgen Roelandts and Dirk De Wolf in a typical bar. I was finally relaxed, even though a VRT chauffeur was waiting for us, Olivier Kaisen and me, in order to drive us to Paris. We slept like logs for a couple of hours in an Ibis Hotel then headed for Montparnasse Station to take a train to Nantes, where a chauffeur of the Chrono des Herbiers organisation came to find us. I was not obliged to impose this marathon on myself, I grant you, but I have always been loyal to this event because I like its organizers. It also enables me to see Joseph Briand, who receives us in his guest house, once again each year. The anecdote is amusing because, on that particular day, I was unaware that, nine months later, I was going to be donning the yellow jersey of the Tour de France in Herbiers! I slept a little in the camping car: I had forced myself to do some basic warming-up on the rollers but I was literally dead. I had only eaten a little rice, I was drained, devoid of strength, even though I still felt OK. Just imagine: David Millar was two minutes ahead of me after ten kilometres!

There, I thought about my previous day's feat again: my mind was already elsewhere but it is clear that my second victory in the Lombardy conditioned the rest of my career and therefore the 2011 season, because this event is certainly the most difficult one of the calendar. I found myself at home again the following day, in Monaco, at around 3 p.m. via Nantes, Lyons and Nice. I was consumed by fatigue, and on the Boulevard du Jardin Exotique where I previously lived, the crates for our future removal were strewn on the ground. On seeing Patricia's well-rounded tummy, I said to myself, at that precise moment, that the true, ultimate happiness was only just beginning.

CHAPTER 2

Alan, My Greatest Victory

The success of a high-level sportsman, especially in cycling, depends not only on his talent, his work, his diet and his professionalism, but also on the private life, the happiness and the serenity that a family life can provide. Alan Gilbert was undoubtedly in a hurry to meet his parents and his champion dad, since the latter had hardly returned from the Vendée when the former decided to arrive in the young couple's life - a few days before the gynaecologist's prediction.

> *'Alan was born on 27 October at 16:32 whereas he was expected on*
> *06 November. I took the bus at eight o'clock in the morning with*
> *Patricia, who was complaining of contractions, and as soon as the*
> *gynaecologist didn't send us home again, I realized that the baby was*
> *going to arrive in the course of the day! I attended the birth, of course,*
> *and I will remember that particular joy all my life: it far transcends*
> *the happiness felt at the time of a victory. Alan spent the first night*
> *with other new born babes and I returned all alone to the flat. I had*
> *a wash; I no longer knew my own name: even going to the baker's to*
> *buy a croissant was a burden! There was no longer any question of*
> *cycling: I didn't want to hear it mentioned: I was in a hurry to live*
> *my paternity and to share my emotions with my nearest and dearest.*
> *When the three of us returned to the flat, I received my mother Anita*
> *and my goddaughter Laura, who had come down from Belgium*
> *during the All Saints' Day public holiday. Surrounded by crates, it*
> *wasn't easy to receive anyone, but everyone understood, even the great*
> *Eddy Merckx and his wife Claudine. I was also visited by training*
> *and racing friends, such as Rebellin, Gerrans, and Steegmans.'*

'Don't Put On Any Weight!'

Only the 'Golden Bike' was missing from the list of prizes collected by Philippe during an autumn that was burdened by obligations. The trophy awarded by the 'L'Equipe' newspaper had admittedly not taken account of the races of October. 'Fleming of the Year, Crystal Bike, French-speaking Community Prize, Sports Personality of the Year', Philippe was inevitably solicited in a vein that he liked less than the actual competition. He above all had to accommodate receptions and meals to which he was unaccustomed.

'It's the period when I have to be careful not to put on weight. I'm obsessed by diet but this preoccupation is as important as a good training session. When I'm not cycling, like in November, I don't eat starchy foods: nor any pasta or rice: I don't want to let myself go on the pretext that the season has been heavy. So I eat light, but I lose all the same a little muscle, which is inevitably transformed into fat. I already know at that moment what is waiting for me in the gym later, but usually, I don't put on much weight and, no matter what happens, I quickly know when there are 500 grams too many or too few: either way, they make a real difference !'

My First Race With My Supporters

If there is one appointment in the year that Philippe wouldn't miss for anything in the world, it is his supporters evening, jointly organized halfway between his native village, Remouchamps, and its local town, Aywaille. A tradition, since time began, on the third Saturday of November, right in the middle of the hunting season (a pastime that he adores) and the Beaujolais Nouveau period. Since he has acquired his supreme fame, it is above all, for the members of his supporters club, an opportunity to approach the local hero, inevitably less available since he has been living in Monaco.

'Rather than being content with a single supper where I invite team mates, a surprise guest or regulars such as Marc Madiot and Dirk De Wolf, we added, last year, a Philippe Gilbert cycle race of about sixty kilometres. Even though it's not the finest period of the year in terms of climate. It was a superb memory because it was my official resumption of cycling! There were more than 200 competitors, and it's always nice to find your supporters around you on bicycles because it enables people to come as families, little and large, young or less young, and to do a few hours of sport. Some of my Omega Pharma-Lotto team mates were at the party. Obviously, it was a bit bizarre at the beginning, but really nice. This day plunged me back me into my first emotions in cycling. With my brother Jérôme, I took part in the excursion known as the "Mare aux Joncs", which runs from Seraing to Stoumont and then goes back down the Amblève Valley. I sometimes took part in it three times a week, on Wednesdays and the two days of the weekend in a band that we called "the Group", quite simply. There was a rule dictated by Albert, the person in charge: to take over for five minutes, not more, but us, we wanted more, we had ants in our pants. The competitive spirit was already present and in the descent towards Remouchamps, just before setting off towards Comblain and Hamoir, we attacked flat out! When I see the children and the teenagers who take part, I'm nostalgic for my youth, it's moving. My pal Michael Delage had tried to organise a plot against me but I quickly saw what he was up to and there, already, I decided to win the race!'

'The evening in the overheated room is the only moment of the year, or almost, where I can share some emotions with the people whom I know, and love. I read only happiness in their eyes and that pleases me because, let's be clear about it, I haven't changed my behaviour in relation to them. They have been loyal to me since the beginning; I owe them much and will never disavow them on the pretext of becoming world number one. Even if I have to repeat the same thing 600 times during the same evening! My friend Sébastien Georis (journalist at the RTBF and coming from Remouchamps himself) can always be relied upon for entertainment. Last year, he had found *an amusing game: he played some radio recordings and I had to guess the event during which they had been made.'*

The Third Crystal Bike

Since the birth of Alan, this was the first time that Philippe had returned to Belgium. On Wednesday, 24 November, he went to collect his third 'Crystal Bike' in a row. With more than 200 points more than his Omega Pharma-Lotto teammate, Jurgen Van den Broeck, fifth place on the Tour, Phil won the vote, not only for his prize, as was underlined by the Minister-President of the Flemish Community, Kris Peeters, but also *'for the example that he represents in Belgium, for the young. This champion always has a smile, he sets objectives and he never disappoints.'* Garlanded, drowned in compliments, including that of Johan Museeuw (*'Since Van Looy, De Vlaeminck and of course Merckx, we have never had a cyclist like him.'*), Gilbert, as usual, did not get bigheaded. *'What interests me above all is to win cycling trophies.'* At Omega Pharma-Lotto, it was harvest time. Mario Aerts obtained the title of best team-member, Marc Sergeant that of best Sports Manager.

> *'I took advantage of the occasion to answer the questions of the journalists who, meanwhile, had assailed me with phone calls in Monaco but I hadn't had time to answer everyone and then, in November, I have fewer things to recount! Then, back to Monaco because the removal was envisaged for 28 November. We were at the end of the lease in our former flat but the workers hadn't finished on the other side! We arrived, Patricia, Alan and I, with our crates and our furniture in the utmost confusion but without ever giving way to irritation. It was a bit like a camp-site at the beginning but, there too, I have kept a good memory of it, even though, for me, the holidays were over: I had started to cycle again a week ago.'*

CHAPTER 3

Training, My Work of Every Day

Philippe, Patricia and Alan had established their headquarters in their new home on the Rock, just a stone's throw from the Monaco Palace and the oceanographical museum that was so dear to Commander Cousteau's heart. The house is only accessible by foot through narrow streets where the sun is full of joy, allowing an azure sky to appear. The work was finished: the interior smells of newness, tranquillity and serenity. So the training had been resumed, while in Belgium, the road services were submerged by an early winter: the country was paralysed by snow.

'This is the main reason for my exile to Monaco and I realise, today, that I can no longer do without the sun, the tranquillity or the peaceful training roads. I don't miss my earlier excursions in the Ardennes, dolled up to the neck in winter clothes. Training should be a pleasure, not a chore. I manage my programme alone and report to Dirk De Wolf, the manager appointed for my Omega Pharma-Lotto group, which was entirely logical. I just have to let him know my schedule every day. At the beginning, in December, I rode for two to two and a half hours on a relatively flat course. I have a group of faithful tourist riders in Monaco, some of whom furthermore are Belgian, who accompany me almost daily because the rhythm and the course suit them. We invariably set off around 9 o'clock in the morning, in the direction of France heading towards Nice and Cagnes, and, before the return, we often have a coffee on the Cape of Antibes or beside the beach in Juan-les-Pins. It's really nice when the weather is fine because there is almost nobody other than locals around. That's another advantage of living in Monaco. Nobody knows you; you're not badgered by anyone, which is very important for your peace of mind. After ten days, I increase to 3 hours of cycling. The ideal is to turn your legs very quickly, from 100 to 120 revolutions per minute. It's very demanding at the beginning but essential for the

heart rate, and for the pure stamina work. In the afternoon, I treat
myself to two-hour body-building sessions in a fitness room that's just
a stone's throw from my home. There, I rebalance the upper part of
the body. This is important after more than a month without any
physical exercise.. Thanks to the tonicity of the exercises, the stature
is restored and it's astonishing to see that the muscle quickly becomes
prominent again after just a few days of body-building. This is a
message for those who suffer in their gyms wondering whether it's all
worthwhile. Yes it is, if it's done properly!'

Team Building in Marche-en-Famenne

Marc Sergeant had chosen the delightful little town of Marche-en-Famenne,
in the north of the Province of Luxemburg, for the first team get-together.
The contrast of climate between the mildness of the Riviera and the cold of
the already established Belgian winter was striking.

'Marc had chosen the "team-building" formula, a little three-day stay in the
Quartier Latin, a splendid establishment in the middle of the town. Many
newcomers had joined in the team during the transfer season and we all had to
introduce ourselves in English. 27 riders assembled in a room, having to stand
up and speak in front of everyone - it's not easy, believe me. It was complicated
for the shy ones, the young ones, like Jens Debusschere, and it was also a catas-
trophe for the sports managers who stammered along in their English. Those
three days were extremely important for bonding, especially with the Germans
who had joined our set-up. The activities were varied, including a Tyrolean
traverse near La Roche, in Jupille (not to be confused with the borough of
the same name, near Liege, famous for its lager), *even though I'm not a fan*
of climbing exercises, suspended in midair. This get-together was great for the
Omega Pharma-Lotto group. I say again, Marc Sergeant had had an excellent
idea.'

It was then time to find the sun again, and milder work conditions. The
team embarked for the first of three training stints in Palma, Majorca.
But, meanwhile, a final obligation was awaiting Philippe in Belgium.

On 19 December, he received - for the second year running - the 'Sportsman of the Year' prize awarded by the sports correspondents. He won it with 50 points ahead of Kevin Borlée, and with 300 more than Philippe Le Jeune. *'I thought that world title won by Le Jeune would be conclusive in the vote but, OK, I was delighted to win the prize.'* On that day, after receiving the trophy from the hands of Miss Belgium, Cilou Annys, Philippe told the journalists that he felt ready for a great season. He hadn't yet realized the importance of his remarks. He also added that he would perhaps enter the Tour de France after being included in the shortlist ... of the 14 riders chosen by Marc Sergeant.

'My Dinner in Barcelona with Marc and Jurgen'

As will be seen later, the relations between the sports manager of the Belgian team and its traditional leader were easy and required few words.

'When we left for the Majorca training stint with Jurgen Van den Broeck (placed fourth in the Sportsman of the Year) and Marc Sergeant, we made a stopover in Barcelona. At around eleven o'clock in the evening, Marc invited us to an exceptional restaurant that he knew. I found the approach very enriching once again, because it was nice to see the team's two Belgian leaders enjoying a meal with their manager, who paid with his own credit card rather than with the team's. That proved to us, in a way, the confidence that he had in us, even the affection that he felt for us. If I confide some little details of this kind to you, it is to show you that the exceptional quality of my season was also built on little things, many of which seemed unimportant but which had major repercussions later on.'

'We then returned to Majorca. The weather was fine but still cold. There was also, usually, a lot of wind. It was consequently important to choose to climb the hillsides by the southern face even if it meant crossing the same one five or six times, because it enabled us to avoid the wind and the cold at one and the same time. There, it was the first

training as a group. We alternated between large and small plateaus in order to develop our power and our strength. Personally, I often pedalled standing up in order to balance the periods with those of sitting on the saddle. At that particular time, I was at a normal level of fitness, below that of some of them who had stopped their season earlier, in September, and who therefore had resumed training before I did. The differences in December between the riders are sometimes huge.'

In the splendid establishment placed at their disposal in Palma, the riders had everything they needed.

'Our head chef accompanied us, which is important because that meant that we could eat whenever and whatever we liked. For me, the formula doesn't change: balanced and light. We also have our childish little customs, I would say, like the baptism of the newcomers, which consists of throwing them into the swimming pool where the temperature, Majorca or not, was still icy at that time. While trying to chuck Pujol Oscar, who however is neither very big nor very heavy, into the pool, several of us fell in as well! Some had picked a water fight or a fruit fight. This time, however, Marc Sergeant was furious, telling us that the owner had placed cameras everywhere and that the culprits would be found. This message calmed everyone down, like kids in a scout camp. During the training, we spent four to five hours on the bike but there were also other activities. We had lots of meetings and photo sessions, and interviews that will be aired when the team is presented. It should be known that each sponsor, important or not, requires photographs with each leader. The same shot in portrait and in profile sometimes has to retaken 60 times and always with a smile for the postcards that will be distributed at a later date! The programme was defined during the meetings. My status entitled me to the enormous privilege of choosing my races and my team mates while others had to accept what they were given. In December, I limit my programme to Liege-Bastogne-Liege, that's cast in stone. It was therefore not yet a question of the Tour.'

Once the first training stint was over, the riders were sent home for the Christmas holidays.

'In winter, generally, I could accept an invitation every day but, in 2010, I refused them all, even a trip to Italy with Thor Hushov, a hunting party and my virtually annual visit to the Bordeaux region to stay with my friend Michael Delage, who is of course a wine connoisseur. I chose only rest with Patricia and Alan, and the training, of course. At Christmas and New Year's Eve, we didn't see anybody: it was a bit monastic but not at all sad, especially as I'm not really that keen on parties.'

2011 arrives, the year of much joy, the scale of which Philippe of course has not the slightest inkling. Before heading back to Majorca for the second training stint, he submits to his ritual.

'My objective is twenty hours of cycling per week, not to mention the couple of hours in the gym. Thor Hushovd often comes with my group of friends and me. That enables us to practise various languages while riding, so it's not by chance if I can get by in several languages. You learn that from contact with others, not inevitably in a course! We attack each other, we enjoy ourselves, and we fight out the sprint. The early part of the year is also when we receive our new jerseys. Mine arrived late. I was horrified when I first met my future tunic. I had recorded on my Facebook profile that Omega Pharma-Lotto was competing for the ugliest jersey of the group. "Vélo Magazine" reproduced the information and the people at Omega Pharma-Lotto were not best pleased. Geert Coeman (the financial manager) was not happy, nor was the person responsible for the design. I was severely told to pull my socks up.... But happily, a few weeks later, Vélo Magazine produced a ranking of the World Tour circuit jerseys and we came last, so thank you Velo Mag! Among everything that you receive, there is a complete range of clothing that you will need during the race or otherwise. As the outfits change each year, I pack some enormous suitcases and send the previous years' stuff to Burkina Faso via my friend Michel, whom you certainly know by sight, as he was the former slater (the man who informs the riders of the race situation via his slate on a motorbike). They like that, because they cycle a lot over there and when I can help, we'll come back to this later, I like to do so.'

'I'm meticulous about my equipment, and about my clothes as well. I often wash them myself, especially the shorts, which age badly if put into a machine, and they become rough in contact with the skin. I also start to intensify my training. Sometimes, I do as many as six hours of cycling per day, and string together many hillsides and changes of rhythm. Around mid-January, I'm already at an interesting level. In Monaco, I'm lucky enough to have the services of a regular physio who used to work in a professional team. He's really good, he has a huge clientele and he comes to your home, which is extremely practical. When training and when racing, I obviously have my trainer, who is Dirk Leenaert, whom furthermore I'm taking to BMC next season. We're as thick as thieves, which is essential at this level.'

'We left for Majorca again for the second training stint. There I had my first, let's say official, meeting with the Belgian and the international press since the beginning of the calendar year. I said the same thing to all the journalists for an hour or an hour and a half, and then the television stations and even some magazine journalists wanted some specific interviews. When training, that's what tires me the most! I'm often asked if I've done any special work on my communication skills. No, but I've improved: when I see the interviews that I gave at the beginning once again, it's clear. I've especially made quite a lot of progress in learning languages, which is crucial when you live in cosmopolitan teams where the basic language for everyone is English. This second training stint went well once again, without a hitch, but I'm starting to have ants in my pants. To be clear, I'm impatient to race!'

CHAPTER 4

My First Victory in the Algarve

Even when success is to hand, a season always has its irritations, those little details, as Philippe puts it, which can make a difference in one sense or another. Marc Sergeant's men were already in Majorca for their second training stint when Philippe openly voiced his regret at not having being selected for the two events in the Emirates organized jointly by Eddy Merckx and the Amaury Sport Organisation (ASO). A few weeks earlier, indeed, a misunderstanding had purely and simply prevented the Omega Pharma-Lotto team from having a presence in Qatar and then in the Tour of Oman. However, as in 2010, both races featured in the Philippe's programme.

'It was a big mistake by the team. It had initially sent Eddy Merckx a pre-list without Greipel or me on it, whereas each team had to delegate at least one leader in order to be selected (Editor's note : which is all the more justified in that these races are part of the continental calendar and can accept only 60% of teams coming from the World Tour). *It was in a way a B Team. Eddy was legitimately very angry: he did not want, to repeat his expression, this tuppenny-ha'penny team. I rang him a few days later to tell him that I was coming to Qatar but it was too late, according to him: the papers had been sent to the International Cyclist Union and nothing could be done about it. I was livid: we had to change all the plans. I had the impression, suddenly, that I was working with amateurs ! I was annoyed with the team's staff but also with Eddy because we have always had good relations. Why hadn't he called me as soon as he had received the list? I would have corrected the error immediately. Happily, I'm not someone who remains annoyed for long. Life goes on, you have to fall on your feet and, as it happens, I had no other choice than to register for the Majorca Challenge. The cancellation of the Qatar and the Oman was especially detrimental for the team-members, because at the beginning of season, it's not easy*

*to find a programme for everyone. We had a selection for the Down
Under Tour, and another envisaged in the Emirates, so we had to
juggle with the calendar.'*

A Visit to the Monte Carlo Rally

Between the second and the third training stint in the Balearic Islands, Philippe
treated himself to a distraction that he is passionate about : motor racing.

*'I had been invited to the Monte Carlo Rally by Skoda. It was
superb: what a spectacle ! It enabled me to meet Freddy Loix, and we
exchanged a few thoughts about our respective sports. I love watching
motor racing, whatever the discipline, and I also like to drive but for
me that happens only very seldom.'*

*'During the first two training stints, I accumulated about 64 hours of
cycling. During the last one, from 23 January to 30 January, I realised
that I was a bit behind my schedule. We had in addition wasted even
more time on photo sessions for the introduction of the team in Eeklo,
at the beginning of February.'*

*'Behind schedule and unhappy with the equipment. There was not
a single identical bicycle: I was able to try them all, but my position
wasn't right. However, and this will surprise many people, but I
had quite a few technical problems this season ! On the subject of the
equipment, I know that this interests the purists, I don't have a bespoke
bicycle, I have "normal" proportions, which enable me to ride on a
standard machine. My training bicycle is heavier, more resistant, the
tyres also, inevitably. We maintain our training bikes ourselves. As far
as I'm concerned, I go to Massimo, the only one who has a cycle shop
in Monaco ! For the design, I take care of it myself. Last winter, we did
a wind tunnel test in the McLaren factory in Manchester, but it was
unbearable rather than interesting. In the service race, we had also
reckoned that there was a real problem with defective settings on our
bicycles. With the first race approaching, that was becoming irritating.'*

For the... Fourth Time in Majorca!

After the traditional introductory press conference in Eeklo in front of a Belgian press panel, the guests, the sponsors who envisage a magnificent season, and the promises that are exchanged, it was time to contest the first race.

Return therefore, for Philippe, to... Majorca, for the fourth time in two months! The Majorca Challenge is a stage race without any official general classification: it is possible to give up on the first day and to ride on the following one, a formula that is liked at the beginning of season. But in 2008, Philippe had fought to win the outright, which furthermore gave him another line on the prize list (two partial victories and the outright). At the beginning of the season, it's always that in the bag. Furthermore, he knows the roads by heart, inevitably.

> 'But the equipment was still not ideal: I changed my bicycle and my shoes practically every day. That said, if you don't make changes in a race like Majorca, it's more annoying if the problem occurs later! I found myself one day in a breakaway group, I wasn't too bad despite my concern for my condition, but I didn't win. Incredibly, the Belgian journalists who were there were becoming impatient. I read in certain newspapers that people were worried about my form. I didn't understand, at that moment, why this pressure was imposed on me from the start. It's true that I often win a race fairly early in the year but I often point out that in 2010, I had had to wait for the Amstel Gold Race before raising my arms for the first time. And in 2009, it was nevertheless in the Giro, during the penultimate stage!'

My First Victory, in the Algarve

'I therefore left Majorca with my morale OK, and with a bicycle more or less in order, but I had, meanwhile, added a race to my programme in order partly to compensate for my absence from Qatar and Oman: the Tour of Algarve.'

In Majorca, it had above all been a question of sprinters. Farrar, Rojas and Fischer had already made their mark, while at the Belgian level, Ben Hermans had brilliantly asserted himself during the third stage. Philippe knows the Algarve perfectly, this splendid region in the south of Portugal where the plateau is generally is very high. During his two previous participations, he had been at a party for Alessandro Petacchi (2007), and then for Alberto Contador (2009). The Man from Madrid furthermore had also asserted himself in 2010 and it was in a very tricky context that he arrived at the start of the 2011 event on 16 February flanked by a pack of Spanish and foreign journalists. Authorized to ride while waiting for the famous decision of the Sport Arbitration Court (SAC), the Spaniard was the absolute star of the media, which suited Philippe perfectly.

On that particular morning, it was raining, the sky was pretty gloomy above those landscapes that are usually bathed in gentle sunshine. Long shorts and long sleeves were essential, not to mention track suits. A really good Belgian race, to some extent, in preparation for the 'Het Nieuwsblad' circuit but without the paving stones! As the day went on, however, the rain eased off. At Omega Pharma-Lotto, they were working for André Greipel, back empty-handed from the Down Under Tour. The German was in a hurry to prove to the Belgian team that he hadn't made a bad transfer.

'The team had put its foot down to contain the day's breakaway group. We had above all located the arrival, which was some 600 metres from the house that Jürgen Roelandt has in the Algarve. Roelandts and Greipel had picked up the pace with the approach of a small hump that preceded the arrival. There, I came out of the group with a kilometre to go. During the time it took for the others to react, the gap had been made. I was content, but no more than that. I vaguely remember having raised an arm, undoubtedly because the time had been awful. I was on the other hand delighted for the team and the team-members in relation to the job done. Once again, I secured the first victory of the season for Omega Pharma-Lotto. In that respect I never understood, when I rode in the Française des Jeux, why the Belgian Lotto and Quick Step teams amused themselves

by counting the points like goals in football, comparing their victory
tables. I've always considered that to be ridiculous.'

'With an arrival at altitude and an against-the-clock on the last day,
I knew that the final general classification would be complicated. But
I had defended the jersey (victory in the Degenkolb sprint during
the second stage) because a leader's tunic earns respect. I had lost it
to Cummings during the evening of the third, mountainous, stage.
On the other hand, André Greipel had won the penultimate stage:
he was delighted, and so were we. We had decidedly not come to the
Algarve for nothing, leaving with two bouquets.'

Tony Martin, the final winner, benefitted from it to turn to account, already,
his great season against the clock by dominating Contador and the others.
But in Belgium, people have been speaking about only one thing for a few
days now: the Het Nieuwsblad circuit and the first potential confrontation between Philippe Gilbert and Tom Boonen refereed by the enormous
foreign stables such as Sky, BMC or Garmin-Cervélo. The tone mounts, the
tension also: we can feel the great season of the classics, Philippe's favourite,
returning at pace.

CHAPTER 5

'The God of the Final Kilometre'

In Belgium, the winter seemed interminable. Admittedly, the enormous layer of snow had gradually left the Ardennes where the fields, whitish and filthy, were desperately awaiting a touch of mildness to become the most beautiful green once again. In Mouscron, the town was in mourning, shocked by the sudden death of François Vanassche, 32, the son of Yves, the well-known organizer of the Tour of Wallonia, and of the Grand Prix of Wallonia inter alia.

> *'I knew Francois well: he had many ideas and a great ambition to follow in his father's footsteps. We had met on several occasions and we kept regularly in touch. I was very shocked, like everyone, by his death. It was during the evening of the second stage of the Tour of Algarve: it took me a while to believe it because I couldn't imagine the disappearance of such an active young fellow. I'll come back to this later, but I was in a hurry to pay him homage by winning the Grand Prix of Wallonia, for his father, his mother, his wife Sabrina and his two young children.'*

With the 'Het Nieuwsblad' circuit approaching, the hullabaloo was going through the roof. The press was packed with full pages where the favourites for the opening race in Belgium were dissected under a magnifying glass. There was a lot of talk about a confrontation between Boonen and Cancellara, two specialists who however have never won this race. Contrary to Philippe, two-time winner all on his own at the end, already demonstrations that were to invoke others. We thronged around the Quick Step and Omega bus on Place Saint-Pierre where umbrellas were a must. The weather was so bad that it didn't encourage the cyclists to be in a hurry to leave their coach, where the heating was appropriate.

> *'At the start of this race, I feel a lot of pressure. When you're leader of*

a Belgian team, that's normal. The sponsors make a meal of it: it's the first excursion of the year for them, and they want to see their jersey in the limelight. This was a very special race, once again marked by technical problems as in Majorca. I lost a lot of energy getting upset by that. Adam Blythe had to do a lot of work to replace me, he was tired and meanwhile, the race was played with the breakaway group that included Jürgen Roelandts, so I didn't have any reason to compete.'

Thus, the marking between the big favourites marvellously benefitted the more daring ones of the breakaway group and, under a cloudburst, the Dutchman Sebastian Langeveld asserted himself over the procession against the only one of the pretenders who had assumed his responsibilities, Juan-Antonio Flecha.

'On that particular day, I gave a guy some pleasure without realizing it. When I returned with Blythe after my technical problems, I was hot and I threw my jacket to a spectator. Unfortunately I had left my goggles in it ! I doubly regretted what I'd done because, after Eikenberg, nothing went right, the breakaway group had more than three minutes, it was finished and I started to get cold. The team car had already gone ahead, so no way of getting a tracksuit: in other words, I was soaked to the skin and as cold as ice at the arrival !'

'I've changed my mind about the earpiece'

It is true that for the first time, following the new regulations, the race proceeded without the support of the famous earpieces. No longer any question, consequently, of communicating with ones sports manager. However, a few months earlier, Philippe had assumed his responsibilities by showing his support for getting rid of the earpiece, unlike most of the cyclists. An approach that undoubtedly was not overly popular.

'I'm working with the son of the president of the International Cyclist Union, Pat McQuaid. Andrew deals with registering me in the rallies

*and I had asked him for his father's e-mail address. I had actually
sent him a text in which I explained my reasons for being against
the earpiece. I'm still convinced that they are unfavourable for the
attackers in the breakaway groups but for the rest, I've changed my
mind: we all make mistakes. Because in view of what happened on
the Het Nieuwsblad circuit, I realised that the officials weren't ready,
and that our federation wasn't either. The return of the slater cannot
just happen from one day to the next. We never knew that the leading
group was three minutes ahead. I now have my doubts on the subject.
Getting rid of the earpiece calls for far more motorcyclists for the race,
just for keeping us informed, as was previously the case. I think that
one solution among others would be to equip only two cyclists per
team, including the leader, which seems to me fair and to go in the
strategic direction desired by the ICU while guaranteeing the cyclists'
safety. But that depends on the vision of each cyclist, and of each
sports manager. As wide a debate as possible would be needed, and a
consensus to be reached unanimously.'*

Langeveld victorious in Ghent, Chris Sutton the following day in
Kuurne, the opening weekend in Belgium had already known better days.
Meanwhile, under the Sardinian sun, the young Sagan was unstoppable; he
was already being spoken about as the favourite for the Milan-San Remo.

'My Anti-Doping Film'

Philippe, for his part, was in a hurry for only one thing: to go
back home. *'I was literally shattered when I arrived in Monaco on
Sunday. I collapsed into my armchair: I had been very cold on the
previous day. I have however always borne such dreadful conditions.
And here, you have only one fear, but it's awful at this time of the
season: to fall ill: that could call everything into question. On that
particular day, I didn't get my bike out - I wouldn't have been able.*

*'On the Monday, I had a long-standing appointment: the recording
of a film for the French-speaking Community. I had accepted a*

*proposal from the Minister of Sport, André Antoine, to take part
in an anti-doping advertising campaign. The images had been shot
close to the Monaco Novotel. The storyboard that had been created
upstream was irreproachable: it was even remarkable. In the images,
I symbolically crush a syringe. Many wonder why I had accepted
this challenge at a time when cycling was gripped by doping affairs,
even though they've been less frequent in the last two years. As a
winning cyclist is a suspect cyclist for most people, you can imagine
the comments when people look at this clip and reckon that I must be
mad - "if ever anything should happen to me". They needn't worry!
I was brought up in cycling by Marc Madiot, a leader of the anti-
doping fight in the peloton. I know that nothing will happen to me.'*

*'I arrived in Italy on 2 March, the day of the mother Anita's birthday,
which is why I remember the date well. My Italian programme
started with the Strade Bianche. A little aside - before continuing in
connection with the travel that is part of our daily lives in the world's
most itinerant sport. I would like publicly to thank Valerie from the
Omega Pharma-Lotto race department for her availability and her
nous. She is committed to finding solutions all the time. However,
in this line of work, we're on the move all the time and the less time
we waste the better. If I have to take four different planes to take
part in a race, I prefer not to go: it's simpler! In the flight proposals,
I always asked for the most direct and the team for the least expensive.
It was logical, but I obtained this privilege all the same. To lose the
least energy and to suffer the least stress is vital for a cyclist. A well
organized trip can let you win a race. I'm not obsessed with luxury,
I'm a simple soul, but my little exception to this truth is the shuttle
by chopper from Nice Airport to Monaco, a fabulous time-saver. And
when the helicopters aren't flying, I call upon a cab driver, always the
same one, whom I've got to know pretty well.'*

'The Italian Paris-Roubaix'

"I didn't know this race, called the Italian Paris-Roubaix. I've
wanted to discover it for ages. We reccied the last 65 kilometres, a
rather rare initiative as an approach to the least known classic, but it
was essential. I located everything thanks to a touring cyclist friend of
Roberto Damiani, our sports manager, who helped us because there
was not yet any race signage, inevitably. With all the team, I reccied
this strange race and, as it happens, I came across the BMCs, my
future set-up. We rode the last 15 kilometres together and I noted
that the best place for an attack was on the last hill but two. I wasn't
the only one to think that! I tested the group a little and I saw the
selection: Ballan seemed not bad to me. On the day of the race, we
do one and two, it's no secret: it explains many things about cycling.
Luck doesn't exist in sport. Reconnaissance, it's like in a car rally.
I locate unimportant things like posts, corners of houses, colours - it's
extremely important. By also knowing that you don't have any road
signs counting down the metres and that on the day of the race there
will be barriers and the public. Everything has to be memorised,
including the turns. I'm lucky, I have a great memory: I retain
everything!'

'On the eve of the race, at the briefing, I had strongly insisted on
our race as a team: to remain grouped more as long as possible. The
problem was that not everyone was yet ready, physically, and I found
myself alone at 15 kilometres from the arrival, so I had to take on the
work from a little too far, I had left my strength in the brawl and it
seemed to me that the BMC were better organised. I won, as I said
it, thanks to my memory of the place. At the top of the hill of Sienne,
what a superb place furthermore, it was necessary at all costs to be in
the lead in order to take the last turn leading to the arenas inside, if
not, defeat was a certainty. Ballan had had to take the outside and
I asserted myself thanks to that manoeuvre. I was especially wary of
Cancellara on that particular day because he was going well and on
a terrain that he obviously liked. I frankly adored it and I'll return
to it. It's old-fashioned cycling, as I love it. I left with a tyre twisted

around my neck ! I rode with it for 40 kilometres then I gave it to a fan at the side of the road. Finally, I regretted it, because I would have liked to have crossed the line with it: that would have been good for the photograph !'

On Sienne's splendid Piazza del Campo, where the view over the vines of Tuscany is breathtaking, there was no photo, precisely, as Philippe's sprint was so exceptional... already. The following day, the pink Gazzetta dello Sport newspaper called Philippe the 'God of the Final Kilometre', with those various emphases and superlatives that only Italians can produce. Phil had left Italy in 2010 with a resounding success in Lombardy: he returned there in 2011 and had an immediate win. In other words, for the local specialists, no further search for the favourite for the Milan-San Remo was required.

CHAPTER 6

Between Two Seas, A Third Victory

Tuscany, towards the end of the winter, was already beginning its spring. The first whitish colours distilled by a really generous sun awake some daisies. Philippe had chosen to remain in Italy to take part in the 'Two Seas Race', the Tirreno-Adriatico, rather than his customary Paris-Nice. A race that was regularly followed by his supporters, in particular by his father Jeannot and his older brother Christian but no matter, they took advantage it to discover the Tyrrhenian coast at Marina di Carrara, where the start of the Italian stage race was permanently installed.

'Before going down there, I had a little time to kill because the team had planned to reccy a part of the Milan-San Remo course, specially for André Greipel. The German wanted to see, inter alia, the coast of Mania. That didn't interest me and there was a bit of 'friction', on that particular day, with my sports managers, who didn't seem best pleased that I didn't want to go and waste my time and especially a lot of energy in kilometres on the roads in a car in order to reccy a classic that I already knew like the back of my hand. I often train on the San Remo coast. The others left in the bus but I didn't remain on my own for long. In Sienna, after my victory, Alessandro Petacchi had suggested that I should come and cycle with him if that interested me. We had known each other more or less for several years and in a trice he had called a pal who served as the motorcyclist. That enabled me to kill time between the Strade and the Tirreno start. I discovered his area close to La Spezia. We rode well together, alternating the difficulties. Alessandro is a charming guy, with lots of class. Since then, we often talk to each other in the pack: it was an encounter that I'll never forget because it was completely unexpected.'

'Not easy to abandon the Paris-Nice'

*'I had taken part in Tirreno only once, in 2005. Because I adore the
Paris-Nice, it was a difficult choice. I liked to cross the Nievre, the
Loiret, and certain regions of France that can only be discovered in a
cycle race. There's often a lot of wind, tricky stages, possible edges, it is
undulating without being mountainous and then when one arrives
in the south on the Vence side, I obviously know the courses by heart.
But that has never been a success for me: it's a bit strange all the same.
On the last few occasions, it was furthermore very cold, the plateau
was extremely spicy, it was complicated to go to look for a prize in an
event where the guys came for the classification, like Contador. I even
had to abandon an event: my legs gave out, and I was ill. That was in
Ardèche. As an aside on the subject, the thing that I hate the most in
cycling is giving up. To imagine taking part in a great Tour in order
to prepare myself and to stop before the end is not my style, unless of
course the body is no longer up for it. I had to do that once against
my will, also, in the Française des Jeux. Marc Madiot had asked me
to stop for three days of the end of the Vuelta in 2007 because he was
afraid that I wouldn't recover enough for the world championships.
It was in Stuttgart, I had been eighth, so I was too short, it was not
a good calculation. The Paris-Nice or the Tirreno-Adriatico served
only as my preparation for the Milan-San Remo. I didn't want to
win there at all costs even though it's difficult for me to hide away in
a race! I chose the Tirreno, in 2011, and then, when consulting the list
of starters, I realised that the plate was very spicy, more so than in the
Paris-Nice!'*

'Greipel's Fall'

In Marina di Carrara, the beaches were deserted. The typical little res-
taurants all along the immense sandy beaches had been closed for several
months, struck by the dust of the sand. It was a little sad but between two
shades of plane trees, the sun was at the start for warming the cyclists who
were prepare the team against-the-clock events. Curiously, whereas the

competitors had come to prepare for the 'Primavera', the organizers had planned this perfectly pointless timed exercise. Around the coaches arranged like multicoloured bars of chocolate, the spectators admired the cyclists with their ear-phones sweating profusely on the rollers. The Sports Managers gave their last instructions: one felt the tension mounting several notches because the team stopwatch events often generate falls.

> 'But for us, it turned into a reccy! At the end of the first lap, I heard a fracas behind me, and some complaints. A fall.. There was an enormous pothole in the road and one of our competitors had taken it. I didn't immediately recognise that it was Greipel but when he got up again, he was badly hurt in the face. We had tried to persuade him to get into the ambulance but he refused. He had done the warm-up on the rollers with us and he wanted to do the start although in a really awful state but, bravely, he took such an enormous lead that he hurt me over 600 metres: it was his own personal way of showing that he wasn't a tourist, and I was very impressed! And then he came to his senses by abandoning in the evening. For him, compared to the Milan-San Remo, it was obviously a catastrophe.'

Omega Pharma-Lotto came eleventh on the stopwatch that was dominated by the Rabobank team ahead of the Garmin and the HTC. It was the Dutchman Lars Boom, having crossed the line in first place for his Dutch team, who received the leader's jersey.

The following day, the race began its crossing of the 'Boot' towards Indicatore, a little village where the organizers had forgotten to detail the pitfalls of the arrival circuit in the road-book. This meant that the riders had to take a tortuous path through the vines where the vehicles scraped the ditches to make sure that they could pass. 'It was madness, very dangerous but if we had been warned, at the same time by the road guide but especially by the guys of our team who were on the spot, this stage could have smiled on me. There was a severe ascent where I could have gone off on my own. Instead of that, considering the pace, I has above all tried not to fall, because it was very dangerous. I didn't like that stage.' At the end of which Tyler Farrar discovered a pilot fish of rare value, the world champion Thor Hushovd in person, who started the perfect sprint for the American!

The next morning, as a matter of interest, but it will have more value later, Valério Piva (HTC) confided in a long interview to the 'Le Soir' newspaper his state of mind on the subject Cavendish at the start of the Terranuova Bracciolini. And he said this: *'Mark should target his objectives and not try what he cannot yet do, like the Flemish classics. I told him to concentrate on the Milan-San Remo, the green jersey of the Tour and the world championship, nothing else'.* The message, it seems, got across loud and clear between Piva and his capricious rider from the Isle of Man, world champion five months later!

At the Perugia arrival, it was the Argentinian Haedo's turn to take his sprint bouquet, to the detriment of Farrar, who however was feeling good about the double. Philippe, for his part, accomplished the kilometres: he needed to, it was vital for what was going to happen.

> *'And I realised that I wasn't yet on top form. On the bumps, for example, I noted that the uphillers like Evans and Scarponi could easily leave my wheels behind. That was a very interesting indicator for me. The Tirreno is in fact a one-week full-scale training course for competition. I measured the work that still had to be done.'*

'I win the queen stage in Castelraimondo!'

In fact, on the Saturday between Narni and Chieti (240 kilometres), Philippe measured himself against Scarponi. In the narrow neck that leads above the splendid city of the Abruzzi, the damage was important. Gesink thought of taking the power there but his downhiller qualities leave something to be desired. Phil, for his part, was well on the pace but in the last round, on the severest part of the slope, Scarponi made a dart... 'as per Gilbert'. Cunego but especially Evans managed to follow him. Philippe was 12 seconds behind: there was really no danger in the warning but only one conclusion: he had to work.

The following day, the weather decided to offer a Sunday rest by leaving a gloomy sky charged with rain. It was not the right day because the road book gave the information, on the subject of those 244 kilometres between Chieti and Castelraimondo: 'e la tappa di montagna della Tirreno'. Unscrambled, it was the queen stage. *'The mileage brought us closer to the Milan-San Remo; it was very interesting for me. There was a long 15-kilometre pass at the top with a metre of snow on the sides. At the bottom of the bump, I was far away, not overly concentrated, Adam Hansen (the Australian teammate) came to find me, offering to take me back up. In five kilometres, we got back among the first 20 but there were still 10 more uphill kilometres ahead of us. At three kilometres from the top, I exploded, I no longer had a teammate, I lost 30 seconds on the best but I knew that I could regain them in the descent. Afterwards, I played poker. We went up and we went down all the time, there were some who were stronger than me in the lead group, Evans and Scarponi, clearly. There was also a breakaway group that I didn't join. On that day, I won the most improbable of my victories because everybody stuck to my wheels, they were waiting for my attack but it didn't come: that's why I waited until the final kilometre before showing my hand. I made a very long sprint, perhaps the longest of the season, and if the two guys who were in front hadn't looked at each other at the moment of contesting the victory, I would never have won. I also had the luck to pass on the right-hand side, and on the 11 cogs without any rough stuff because, for the same price, I would have been squeezed against the barriers. At the arrival, I was the first to be surprised but very happy because the feat had value, I could feel it. Furthermore, my supporters from Belgium were there, I recognised in particular my father and André, from the "Cheval Blanc" in Remouchamps, waving a Belgian flag bearing my effigy: it was great! Roberto Damiani was screaming with joy into the radio, because for an Italian sports manager, to win a queen stage like that one was worth a fortune.'*

The unhappy Wouter Poels of the Vacansoleil team couldn't get over it. Escaped from an interminable breakaway, he believed that the world was collapsing when he saw the Gilbert's bicycle crossing the line. In the press room next to a podium, where the cold was increasingly intense, the Italian journalists were dumbfounded. For them, it was clear; Gilbert had put the bar very high for the Milan-San Remo. The likes of Freire, Cavendish, Hushovd and company were forty-five minutes behind their Belgian rival in that stage. How would they be able to compete with Gilbert on the Primavera? Philippe's answer was unequivocal. *'To win the Milan San Remo, one need luck and patience. For me, my objectives are more remote, at the Tour of Flanders and the Liege-Bastogne-Liege.'* That same day, Thomas Voeckler won the final stage of the Paris-Nice in pouring rain and Tony Martin the final classification.

Gilbert however was the front page news. One will note on the way that on that particular day he marked his eighth success in Italy after two Tours of Lombardy, two Tours of Piedmont, the Coppa Sabatini, a stage of the Giro and the Strade Bianche. In reality, all that he was really missing to complete this idyllic tableau was ... the Milan-San Remo.

On the Monday, in Macerata, the Evans-Scarponi duel continued but this time it was the Australian who dominated the sprint. It is not yet question, at the time, of a transfer for Phil to BMC, nor of a victory in the Tour for Cadel, but contrary to other candidates for the Tour de France, it could be seen that Evans was particularly concentrated and already in tip-top form. On the last day, in San Benedetto del Tronto, the organizers chose an individual against-the-clock event to bring matters to a close. In relation to Evans, Scarponi obviously had no chance of worrying him. The Italian how-ever clung on in a stopwatch event largely dominated by Cancellara ahead of Lars Boom, whereas Evans quietly managed his final victory. Philippe, for his part, was angry. *A complete failure, I was really cross with myself. And entirely my own fault. I had chosen a too intensive warm-up on the rollers and when I made a dash, I was already spent, I felt that it wasn't right.* 54th, Phil nevertheless finishes ninth in the final Tirreno-Adriatico classification. He obtained, also, his first World Tour points for the UCI world classification. Their crucial importance will be seen later.

CHAPTER 7
The Indomitable Primavera

When the lights go out over the Adriatic where the resort towns are still sleeping their prolonged hibernation, it is, for the riders, a time to wait. The interminable wait between the end of the Tirreno and the start of the calendar's first great classic, the Milan-San Remo.

'The most tedious journey, by coach, is indeed the one that takes us back to Milan. It's long, you have to kill time, to try to rest. Once I arrive at the hotel in the remote suburbs of the Lombardy capital, I'll ride with the "Taticci", some friends of Roberto Damiani who have discovered a circuit of about fifteen kilometres that we do several times, the last ones behind a scooter. That enables the speed to be increased, because speed is the watchword of the Primavera.'

The sports pages of the dailies are already dissecting the tactics, the favourites and the team play at the approach of longest classic of the calendar, the one that perhaps generates the most nervousness. During the Tirreno-Adriatico, I also had the impression that the favourites had done everything to release the pressure, to discharge it on to their opponents. *'Every day, I saw Freire pick himself up when things became complicated but that's something that I cannot do when I can win a race. The problem in my view was to counter the Garmin-Cervélo which was presenting three favourites with Farrar, Hushovd and Haussler.'* The American team had indeed stood out at the time of quoting the favourites, as well as the Dutch Rabobank formation, which had emerged from the winter with an impressive collection of bouquets as varied as those of Robert Gesink in Oman, of Langeveld in the Nieuwsblad or of the team timed event in Marina di Carrara.

The Milan-San Remo, it's not the Tour of Lombardy but a race with its own particularities, where bluff is perhaps, or even certainly, the most required quality. So who? Haussler had fallen in the Paris-Nice, Petacchi, like McEwen, hadn't finished the Tirreno; Sagan, designated as the ogre of spring after the Tour of Sardinia, had disappeared from circulation, Boasson Hagen had been invisible in the Tirreno, Boonen had competed while he was ill, and Greipel had thrown in the towel on the evening of the timed team event! Tony Martin and Cadel Evans, respectively winners of the Paris-Nice and the Tirreno-Adriatico, had already ruled out their participation in the Primavera. Can one include the climbers like Scarponi, Basso, Cunego or Gesink, very much at ease during the 'Race of Two Seas'? In this context, the only rider whose name was winning unanimous support during the pre-match discussions, as one would say in football, was still Philippe.

'On the day before, at the briefing, since Greipel was restored, the instruction was to protect us both, which appeared logical to me. It also took some of the pressure off me. Olivier Kaisen for his part was told to set the pace and to prevent breakaways. It was misty, as usual, at the start. It's nevertheless the race which makes us start the earliest, it's special, a bit grey and magical at the same time. Each year, I tell my team mates to be wary of the railway lines which we must either skirt or cross during first kilometres but, each year, there are falls, sometimes severe. In my opinion, the peloton is still half asleep! However, if there was ever a race where sleeping is not recommended it is that one. Its monotony can lead to distraction and when one arrives on the Riviera peppered with its greenhouses of carnations, it's there that ones vigilance has to be doubled. For a few years now, the organizers have thus added a huge difficulty beyond the Turchino to cream off the best of the peloton even more, the La Manie hill. It was raining, it was foggy, and the conditions were really dreadful. Especially, there was a great deal of nervousness, which was rather unusual. The expression "to rub" is often used in cycling, but here, it was at the limit of aggression. I hadn't wanted to take any risks, I had let myself fall behind a little and then I had a lot of luck. An enormous fall occurred, and I passed between the bicycles. I had in particular seen Thor Hushovd on the ground. They were everywhere. I was convinced that I would return in the descent because, considering the circumstances, it was better to ride in front. But I also had to take a breather, that ascent had been complicated. In the descent, moreover, there was a kind of freezing rain, it beaded on the*

*hairs of the arms ! Freire had fallen at a hairpin bend, slippery and
steep, that had split up the group even more but fortunately, I had
had good tyres. I knew that there had been some damage among my
rivals but I hadn't yet had time to take stock.'*

Take stock? For the first time for several years, the Milan-San Remo had been
decapitated of two thirds of its sprinters whereas the peloton had not yet
climbed any of the 'Capi'. Hushovd, Farrar, Freire, inter alia, were no longer
there. For Philippe, an opportunity to be grasped, the finest ever, perhaps.

*'I had to toughen up in front. I was riding with the Katushas and
the BMCs in particular in order to establish the break definitively.
Boonen was also at the party. I can assure you that I had no time to
look at the seaside landscape. We rode in Indian file; I think that
I remained at the wheel of the same rider, Ballan in fact, for 40
kilometres. Mentally, it's a difficult exercise, because the hours of
cycling, although you wouldn't think so, accumulate. The slightest
lapse of concentration and it's all over. Behind, I knew that the others
were practically two minutes away, that they had therefore abdicated.
At one moment, Marc Sergeant told me in the earpiece that only
Scarponi had counter-attacked in the Cipressa. Despite his climber
qualities and his evident form, I found it hard to see him returning.
I was ascended the Cipressa at a very good tempo when I saw Scarponi
approaching me, saying: "See you on the Poggio". I was gobsmacked !'*

The Poggio, that long four-kilometre snake that winds between the greenhouses and the single-storey houses of another age perched on the hill.
There, the legend is written, it belongs to the history of the bicycle like
eternal arbiters. It is, say the Italians, the property of Eddy Merckx (seven
victories !) who descended it so quickly that it ought to be immunized by
the good offices of the splendid Notre Dame de la Garde chapel that watches
over the Riviera. For the riders, it is a hallowed place, like that of Grammont,
a secular homage that deserves respect despite having been attacked by
several earthquakes. Besides, one shouldn't say 'the' Poggio: that's an
error of syntax because Poggio is one of the five hamlets of San Remo and
therefore a little village. The ideal is therefore quite simply to say: Poggio.

Philippe knew this difficulty as well as that of his childhood, La Redoute in Remouchamps.

> 'It's very special, not steep enough for my liking. With its enormous quantity of hairpins, you sometimes come to a standstill. I already tried to attack it practically on foot, in the middle, at the end, and I think that I've explored its every possibility. This time, considering all the same that some of the sprinters were missing, I was more patient.'

Because in front, the breakaway group was approaching Poggio ahead of the favourites, or at least what was left of them. Chainel and Offredo from the FDJeux were particularly active but it was a Belgian who would set things alight on the last third of the slope: Greg Van Avermaet. The new BMC recruit took his chance and jumped into the lead on the famous left-hand hairpin. Behind him, only Vincenzo Nibali had tried, twice. Van Avermaet was descending alone, also, but behind, the chase was led by Cancellara, with phenomenal skill. *'I was well placed when Marcato fell right in front of Ballan in a turn to the left, I had to deviate to avoid him and that cost me both time and energy. Once in the valley, Offredo tried again: he was really good that day. For me, the troop review was easy, I saw that Goss was sticking to everything that moved and I understood that if I wanted to win, I had no choice but to try my luck in front.'*

Pozzato's 'Treason'

Pippo Pozzato is a veteran of the Monegasque Rock where his transalpine show-off look is as well-known as his pedalling prowess. It wasn't rare, until that 19 March 2011, for the Tuscan to train with Philippe but, since the last hectometres of Milan-San Remo, the two men had preferred to avoid each other. *'When I left at 2,000 metres after having countered Offredo, I was well in the pace and it was Pozzato who had filled the hole on me. It was after reviewing the images that I reckoned that he had only ridden to make me lose since he had behaved as a teammate. But as a teammate of whom? There was no longer any one from Katusha in the group of*

survivors. Instead of trying to overtake me, he could have given me
some relief me and who knows if we couldn't have gone to the end.
It was not the first time that Pozzato had acted like this with me, he
had also already upset me in the Paris-Tours. In fact, we all played
the game of Matthew Goss, the only sprinter of the batch who, despite
his isolation, had superbly benefitted from the circumstances. He was
the fastest and therefore the strongest, and that's the way that things
have to be understood in cycling. It's clear that the scenario of that
Primavera with the peloton cut into two or almost at La Manie was
favourable for me, I perhaps let slip a great chance of winning it but I
had absolutely no regret, except for Pozzato's manoeuvre.'

At the end of the car park that serves as the arrival in the Milan-San Remo,
Philippe managed nevertheless to regain his strength as a sprinter and to
obtain third place behind Goss and Cancellara. As a matter of interest, the
Australian was the first winner since Tchmil (1999) to come out of the Paris-
Nice rather than the Tirreno-Adriatico.

Waited for by Patricia and the little Alan who had been present at
the arrival at the end of the car park in a cul-de-sac that serves as a
curious exit from the Primavera, Philippe was much applauded on
the podium while some raindrops appeared on the roadway. *'I had*
however had the circumstances and a good team, with Reynes and
Roelandts at the end but OK, it's a classic that I've always dreamt
about but one that I still haven't won. It will in any event remain in
a corner of my mind! On the day after the San Remo, it's a tradition
that I won't cut, I take part in the Round of Aix-en-Provence, a nice
rally. It's beautifully organised. I went there with Thor Hushovd
who was waiting for me where he lives on the other side of Monaco
but I arrived 25 minutes late at his place because I had been blocked
by a cross-country race in Monaco in which Prince Albert II was
taking part. That didn't prevent Thor from winning the race, on the
Boulevard des Belges, where I myself finished third. It was Thor's first
victory with his world champion's jersey. Admittedly, it was not at the
end of an official race but I really felt well that it did him some good,
he was happy. In a word, so was I !'

CHAPTER 8

'On the Bosberg, my major mistake of the season'

Third in San Remo, winner of a stage in the Algarve, the Strade Bianche and a stage in Tirreno, Philippe was on track with the approach of the month of truth, namely April. *'I was at 85% of my best form when leaving San Remo, if one really has to look for figures. That in any event is what it felt like. My idea was already, at that moment, to be imperatively on top form for the Liege-Bastogne-Liege, not to neglect any detail, to be absolutely up to scratch. On the day after the Round of Aix, I accorded a long interview to Laurent Bruwier (RTBF) who used it to raise several subjects in connection with the classics. An appointment that was agreed a long time ago. Choosing your dates is a luxury but I believe that, in the light of the heavy programme with which the cyclists are faced, this was the best moment. I'm not an absolute fan of interviews, especially on television. It's a shop window, you are exposed to the whole world and I'm increasingly this oppressive desire of the media to slither on to private ground. What's the point? I was training calmly: two hours on Tuesday, a little more on Wednesday but the weather wasn't good. I had wanted to delay my return to Belgium for the Flemish races campaign as long as possible. In Monaco, I have my programme, I eat what I buy and prepare, and I have my own masseur. I also look at the Sporza website where I study my opponents' performances and form. As of the Wednesday of the "Through the Flanders" in Waregem, I had seen what I had needed to see.'*

In Waregem, the sun was on hand to greet the return of a stranger, Nick Nuyens, known as the "Sniper" for his particular way of winning races when it was not expected of him. The strangest transfer of the winter *mercato* with his transfer to Saxo Bank brilliantly benefited from the hesitations of Garmin and Leopard in a race which they seemed to dominate. Following the example of the courageous Frederic Amorison who would not have stolen the victory, Nuyens emerged a few lengths before the massive sprint, grace undoubtedly to a lack of earpiece. The race was splendid, in any case, and promises to continue to be so, but what is a certainty is that Fabian Cancellara seems to do exactly what it wants in the Flemish mountains where already the smells of party, chips and beer were mounting for a dozen devil-may-care days. In Catalonia, Alberto Contador completed the Saxo Bank's party by winning the queen stage of that Spanish race that counts for the World Tour.

It will be noted in passing that the Nuyens's victory in Waregem filled an absolute Belgian vacuum, since in 2010, except for Rosseler's success in the Brabant Arrow, the Belgians had brought strictly nothing back from the Flemish campaign. A real disaster. And this time?

'The best table of the season'

'I had joined the team in the D'Hulhaege Hotel in Deinze. I mention this name because this is by far the place where one eats the best during the entire cycling season. The owner is a cycling fan, of course, and in the kitchen, he has gold in his hands. He prepares set meals especially for us. I had chosen to contest the Ghent-Wevelgem rather than the E3 Grand Prix quite simply for the allocation of World Tour points that didn't exist in Harelbeke (at the time), which is completely stupid. Because I already had this place of world number one in mind. I had scored points in Tirreno, my third place in San Remo enabled me to take some more and I think that it would be ridiculous not to benefit from the Ghent-Wevelgem. Even if, in brackets, this challenge brings me absolutely nothing, not even recognition. There is no distinctive jersey for the leader (Editor's note: at the request of the World Tour teams, it should be specified) nor any financial reward. When that happens in tennis, Formula 1 or golf, it's distinctly more gratifying!'

The mishmash of the status of the Ghent-Wevelgem and the E3 Grand Prix became a hot potato in the Flemish press. Patrick Lefevere denounced the absurdity of the system because he was obliged to register his leader Tom

Boonen in the Ghent-Wevelgem and not in the E3 GP that the man from Antwerp has already won on four occasions. Quick Step deprived Boonen of his favourite race because, at the time, the team's World Tour classification was not brilliant (18th). And as the order of the vehicles for the Tour of Flanders then the Paris-Roubaix is allocated by this classification, the Belgian team must, as a matter of urgency, wake up. The spectators will not have to regret it: on the Saturday, Cancellara flew over the E3 in a exercise of absolute domination which nauseated the opposition and, on the Sunday, Boonen scapes over the Wevelgem line to impose himself on the sprint as he had done at the same place in 2004. And Philippe? He put everyone in the red as of the first ascent of Mount Kemmel by climbing it on foot right to the top without tolerating the slightest opposition.

> 'It was very odd as a race, nothing happened in it, as if the clemency of the weather prohibited any breakaway On that day, I understood that it was preferable for me to ride for Greipel, which I did in spite of a puncture at the bottom of second Mount Kemmel . I had to return later on the others. My emphatic relays, thereafter, served the cause of the German. Up to 1,500 metres from the arrival, I gave my all to put him in an ideal situation: he finished third. Close, but he didn't win. That day enabled me at the same time to shut the traps of certain critics whom I had read, according to whom I never devote myself for a teammate.'

'I'm ready to assume the role of favourite'

The tendencies become apparent, in any case, with the approach of the Tour of Flanders: Boonen, Cancellara, Gilbert and Nuyens have all shown their teeth. Omega Pharma-Lotto admittedly had no bouquet but it placed Roelandts in the E3 (second) and Greipel at Wevelgem (third). Philippe also cast an attentive eye on the results of the international Rally in Corsica won by Frank Schleck. Victory in the Rally is always an interesting pointer with regard to the Ardennes classics. Philippe Chevallier (UCI) on a visit to the E3 GP, submitted on his side an extremely positive report to the International Cyclist Union. A few months later, the race was also to obtain its World Tour status on condition of being contested on the Friday, two days before the Ghent-Wevelgem.

Unlike other years, many favourites of the Tour of Flanders decided not to take part in the Three Days of La Panne. Philippe had 'only' the Ghent-Wevelgem in his legs as an immersion on the paving stones before the Round. Would it be enough?

> 'I called it a day because I had a huge season before me. If I can avoid using my mental energy unnecessarily, I do so, because the Three Days require special attention: the terrain is propitious for falls. And then, how to explain this state of happiness, I feel good and the more the days advance, the more I envisage the role of favourite for the Tour of Flanders. Much more than for the Milan-San Remo, even though it's my favourite, insofar as other parameters than pure sporting qualities come into play. Punctures and falls are more probable in a race like the Round than in Liege. But in a prize list, a Tour of Flanders, that counts. In 2010, I hadn't approached the Round under the best conditions. I wasn't on top form physically; I weighed three kilos more than my Liege-Bastogne-Liege weight. I made third at the sprint but I was far from the Cancellara-Boonen duel. That time, I had the feeling that I could get much more closely involved in the brawl. I left San Remo where, with a little luck, I could win. I'm therefore in an excellent disposition. The big favourite is Cancellara, nobody other. He's like Schumacher at the time when he was dominating F1: the others, including me, get to the start while hoping to surprise him. It's a fine challenge, because if it's not the Swiss who wins, Sunday's winner will be talked about for a long, long time. He will, no matter what happens, have pulled off something exceptional. At that moment, the Swiss has better than me physically. I'll therefore have to be smart, find strategies with the other teams. It is in any case likely to be animated and I adore that!'

> 'When I arrived from the FDJeux at Lotto, I reckoned the Tour of Flanders was important because, in my new team, they spoke only of that, as of the winter. Even if the new cards to be dedicated for

the 2011 season weren't ready ! I felt that my supporters were a little disappointed !'

The Bruges central square was crammed, of course, on that Sunday, 02 April. The orchestra in front of which the riders had to process for the protocol signature awoke those who were still asleep. The clemency of the sky prefigured a new Round in the sun. The atmosphere, unique in the entire cycling season, from that start to the prestigious scenery, added to the illusion of a legendary day. *'For me, it started with a brake problem when going to sign, but I'm beginning to get used to it ! The guard of honour made by the people when you go to register is impressive, as if you were doing a lap around a packed stadium. I felt an ovation, more than usually. I also knew that my fan club was at the party. That's very important for me. My brother Christian takes care of it and I know their itineraries, so I know where and when I'll be able to see them. I recognise them and, when I can, I signal to them. Since I was a rookie, they are the same, really loyal, including my uncle Guy who seldom misses a race. The team had invited Simon, my sister's son, as a good-luck mascot. Omega Pharma-Lotto had applied a lot of pressure, there were stacks of VIPs walking hither and thither, and an unusual degree of stress was felt within our formation.'*

'Adam Blythe, perhaps my successor'

A few days earlier, Philippe had insisted on the selection of Adam Blythe. In view of the Englishman's work in the Ghent-Wevelgem, Marc Sergeant did not hesitate for a second and furthermore declared: *'Adam is young but he's not afraid of anybody.'* Phil, for his part, was delighted.

'His assignment was to shelter me for 180 kilometres. Which he did very well with wide open eyes: he was impressed by the crowd. I had pushed him to go as far possible once his job was finished so that he would become tougher, have that distance in his legs, because this boy could win the Tour of Flanders one day. When I told him that he had more talent than courage, he was upset, and then he understood

*that if he worked before thinking of the money, he could have a
really successful career. I take him with me to BMC because I also
wanted to take care of him, of his destiny. Blythe is like Vanendert: he
doesn't need to speak to me to understand. A glance and it's OK, it's
a complicity that doesn't happen from one day to the next, it requires
work.'*

While Blythe was protecting Phil from the wind, while he was anticipat-
ing the braking, his leader benefited from it from time to time to show
that, on the mounts, he was the strongest, in particular on the Koppenberg,
where the others' tongues were hanging out. Ahead, the Frenchman Sylvain
Chavanel dared to make a crazy wager in his favourite race in the world. He
was the only survivor of the final breakaway group. *'Then at 47 kilometres
from the arrival, I changed the rear wheel. I remember the place; it wasn't far
from Peter Van Petegem's home. I was not done for, as they said on television.
I changed the wheel because there was more asphalt at the end; I needed more
pressure* (8.5 kilos) *for the end.'* At the same time, Hushovd attacked from
on the Leberg side. Boonen could no longer resist, he passed him and took
Cancellara with him. There was consternation among the followers: why was
Boonen riding behind his teammate Chavanel as Devolder had done two
years earlier, always behind the Frenchman? This offensive played into the
hand of Cancellara, who deposed Hushovd then Boonen before swooping
down on a flabbergasted Chavanel.

*'For me, I thought that it was lost. I had to pass an impressive file of
guys but, with the help of my team mates, I didn't panic, except that
if we were the only ones to ride, it would become impossible. Then…
the BMCs started, that was organised even if it was that it was said
that Cancellara and Chavanel kept the same rhythm, it would be
complicated. My speedometer often displayed 60 kph, I told myself
that it was impossible for them to keep going so quickly much longer.'*

In fact. And then to the general surprise, the Swiss suffered from cramp on
the asc of the Wall of Grammont where he had disgusted Boonen the previous year. Consternation. On the famous Wall, the strongest was still Gilbert,
coming from the back. Everytinghad to be redone not only for Cancellara

and Chavanel, but also Boonen, who was at the party. *Far too many people for my liking. Finally it was as I thought, which is why I calculated my coup on leaving the Bosberg. I felt strong, so why not have a go? Afterwards, I say it with much humility, that expense of energy was my greatest error of the season. I often however have a good feeling but on that occasion, I mistakenly presumed my strength, the kilometres that I still had to cover, and my opponents' resistance.. I was however supported by the public in that long part of the home straight towards Meerbeke. Should I have waited until half of the hill of Bosberg before attacking? Could I have waited for the sprint with Boonen in the circuit? I don't know but this failure encouraged me, for example, to work my against-the-clock more in future. I had also perhaps spent a lot of energy getting into Grammont after changing my wheel. In the last kilometre, I was a little dry; I couldn't do any better. In the sprint, I couldn't stand on the pedals, I could no longer get off the saddle and as there was never any collaboration in the group, it attacked from every direction, I couldn't ride behind everyone.'*

And who emerged without practically having shown the tip of his nose? The 'Sniper' Nick Nuyens, of course, ahead of Chavanel and Cancellara, the pair who had animated the essence of the Flemish debate.

Ninth whereas he made a strong impression from one mount to another, Philippe was very disappointed. He was not to say so on arrival, charging into the bus to recharge his batteries for a few minutes before facing the press and distilling some polished analyses to it, which were felt to be far from spontaneous. *'Actually, I was really cross with myself! I had the feeling of having wasted an opportunity. At the same time, that evening in my bed, the images of Geelong 2010 returned to me, that of a breakaway in Liege, also, when Andy Schleck had deposed me in the La Roche aux Faucons, of the Leuwen championship of Belgium de Leuven when I had left from a long way away. My only consolation was that I had done my race as I had hoped to, to have measured that my condition was clearly improving and not to have done like many others, to ride against Cancellara. I never ride against anybody; I prefer to ride with him, in a breakaway. This attitude perhaps helped me, three weeks later, in relation to the Schleck brothers in the Liege-Bastogne-Liege.'*

CHAPTER 9

The Brabant Arrow as an Aperitif

Bjarne Riis, the Saxo Bank team manager must have a rabbit's foot in Meerbeke. Winner the previous year with Cancellara, there he was drinking champagne with his Belgian recruit, Nick Nuyens, one year later. A rider from Philippe's generation who had crossed swords with his compatriot, in particular in the Grand Prix of Wallonia, then who, unlike Gilbert, had had a far less prolific period. 'Why Nuyens rather than me?', Philippe wondered when he joined his team in a little hotel in the centre of Ninove where Marc Sergeant's men customarily shared a meal after the race.

> '*I took my shower and then I left; I was too disappointed. Dirk Leenaert, my trainer, drove me to Lille where I took a plane for Nice. I was tired, I needed to clear my mind and go into my cocoon. In the plane, I drew up my balance sheet of the Flemish campaign: it was less good in terms of results than the previous year (two podiums in Wevelgem and in the Tour of Flanders where I had come third in 2010) but I was leaving the classics without injury, without disease and without a fall, with an even more keenly honed motivation because I told myself, in the final analysis: if you didn't win, it means that you'll have to train more.*'

In the world rankings published in the Monday afternoon, Matthew Goss was still on top, Philippe was 10th. In the Grand Prix of the Scheldt, the riders of the Flemish classics did their final duty before taking a first period of rest. On the Antwerp city square, also sunny, the boss of the Tour de France, Christian Prudhomme, came to visit the organizers. Between his coffee and his croissant, he said: *'I've seldom seen so much quality and intensity at the start of the season classics. The Milan-San Remo was enthralling, the Tour of Flanders exceptional, and I reckon it's not going to stop!'*
His reflection was premonitory: it embellished the prospects that were awaiting us.

'Phil, you too can do the treble'

'For my part, I had already forgotten. On the Tuesday I rode and from now on I choose, more specifically than usual, some difficult hills in the hinterland, above Menton in particular. I've reduced the duration of my training sessions but I've improved their quality. So I have a 14-kilometre pass that I go up into each day, generally flat out in order to create some pain. I also vary my route, sometimes going to Italy, there are things to be done on that side above Vintimille, Bordighera and San Remo, of course. There, unlike the basic training sessions in winter, I'm often alone, except that this year, I've accompanied Davide Rebellin. He's a cyclist with whom I've always got on well, despite what's happened to him (two-year suspension for doping). From the first day of his suspension, he has never stopped riding. I was impressed by his motivation, his courage. Davide is also an uphill acceleration specialist: we often exercise together. I clearly remember that during that week, he told me: "Phil, you too can do the treble". Rebellin, indeed, had done the famous Amstel-Arrow-Liege treble in 2004.'

During that time, the competitors for the Ardennes were preparing for the Tour of the Pays Basque, a formula that Phil dislikes. *It's too hard, I've never liked that option.* Andreas Klöden won the general there, and Bennati dominated the sprint on the circuit of the Sarthe. In Schoten, Mark Cavendish respected to the letter the programme that Valério Piva had concocted for him. Four years after revealing himself in those same Antwerp suburbs, he flew over the sprint in front of the revelation of the start of the season in this category, Galimzyanov, and Hutarovich, one of Phil's former team mates at the FDJeux. At the arrival, it was chaos, a collective fall not only put Farrar and his friend Weylandt on the ground, but also Boasson Hagen. For Phil, this information was important: with three fractured ribs, the Norwegian was out for six weeks whereas he had been presented as a potential customer for the Ardennes.

On the other hand, in the Pays Basque, some great names were shining: Samuel Sanchez won the queen stage and Joaquin Rodriguez, the outgoing world number one, came to power. The two Spaniards are, undoubtedly, future adversaries. Far, far from Monaco, in the North, the riders ate dust at the time of the traditional reccy of the paved sectors of the Paris-Roubaix. On that occasion, 'Le Soir' had met with Marc Madiot for a long interview. Phil's first mentor among the professionals and the former double winner of the 'Hell of the North', expressed himself with his usual verve on the subject of him whom he had always called his foal. *'He's not bad at this start of the season. When he wins a big race, I immediately text him: we're often in touch, I was at his wedding, and he was at mine His greatest victory was his second Tour of Lombardy. He had impressed me because he had had to digest the disappointment of the Australian event. That's an enormous quality that he has, this ability to rebound. I can't judge his performance in Geelong, I wasn't there. Hushovd is a fine world champion but Gilbert would have been superb too ! I understand that he isn't taking part in the Paris-Roubaix this time, even though he's at ease in all of the one-day races. Once he's got it in mind to win the Liege-Bastogne-Liege, he's right not to come here. He is victim of the staggering of the calendar because it's hard to be on top form in both races. The ideal would be that he wins the Big One, very quickly, and therefore this year, in order to concentrate on a Flanders-Roubaix string next season. I think that he'll be at the top in Liege because I haven't yet seen the great "Phil "in the classics, especially not in the Tour of Flanders where his "spurt" was not yet refined.'*

Marc's analysis has the virtue of clarity because few know Phil as well as he does. *'And he was right in every respect. That's why I continue to string the passes together, to work on my explosiveness.'*

Even deprived of its best rider, while Tom Boonen had some incredibly bad luck in the Paris-Roubaix, Belgium was surfing on the wave of success in the classics. After Nuyens's victory in Meerbeke, it was Johan Vansummeren's turn to offer his fiancée Jasmine a triumph as a proposal of marriage. There again, the marking on Cancellara's shorts had disturbed the race. Benefiting from the marvellous support of his teammate, Thor Hushovd, who however absolutely wanted to win that classic, Vansummeren won the finest race of its career. And when the lights of the Roubaix velodrome were turned off, the Belgians had already begun to dream of a prolongation of the state of grace with Philippe Gilbert. The more so as, at Omega Pharma-Lotto, there was no great joy nevertheless. The Round and the Paris-Roubaix had been failures, one must call a spade a spade, even though Roelandts (14th) had achieved an excellent Paris-Roubaix.

'On the Sunday of the Paris-Roubaix, I saw only the last 40 kilometres because I had imposed a very long day in the passes on myself, usually of six or six-and-a-half hours. But I saw what had to be seen, and the breakaway was made. I was right behind Jürgen Roelandts who was in the right place and then when Vansummeren left, I was also right behind him, I was simply afraid that Bak and Tjallingi would enter the peloton.'

On the Monday, it was Cancellara who dethroned Goss from the first rung of the world classification. Cold comfort for the Swiss. Phil, for his part, had dropped to the 16th place, which was logical as he hadn't raced.

'For the first time since his birth, Patricia and I went back up into Belgium with Alan. We did the journey in two stages, because 1,200 kilometres in a car before a race is never ideal, and even less so for the baby. I spent the night in Haasrode where I had joined my team mates before the Brabant Arrow. At the briefing, I asked that the discussions should be closely monitored. I had a bad memory of the previous year when the breakaway group had gone off a long way ahead. Despite a pretty sustained pursuit, we hadn't got into the leading group. I was glad to see my team mates again, even though I had worried about them every day, about their programmes, and about the quality of their training. I didn't want to neglect any detail before the ten most important days of my life.'

There it is, the famous 'spurt'

In Leuwen, the sun had arrived early and the terraces near the signature podium were open. There was a lot of conversation about Philippe's leanness, about the rippling muscles that were showing beneath his tunic. His face, also, was radiating serenity.

'I had liked this race with its new course the previous year and when it failed to make my list of winners (second in 2008) where Museeuw, Bartoli or Freire

had taken the bouquet, I said to myself, why not me? The race had proceeded exactly as I had imagined. There had indeed been a breakaway group with enough dangerous elements (Leukemans, Hoogerland, Zingle, Tankink, Geslin and Devenyns). At 50 kilometres from the arrival, I left the group and bounced on to the pavement to avoid the cobblestones. I remember having closed the 18- second gap in the space of the slope. Everyone was surprised by my gesture on the pavement: it was often shown again on television. But it saved me some precious time: my old mountainbiker reflexes had served me well!

Actually, the effort was particularly impressive. The famous "spurt" that Marc Madiot had mentioned was well and truly there. With the number 51 on his back, specific to the myth developed by Eddy Merckx in the 1969 Tour for the 51st edition of the Brabant Arrow, Phil now only had to wait.

'The race was done for with such a group in front, it was finished, but above all the tempo had to be ensured. Hoogerland was doing very badly in his supported leads, I felt that he wanted to toughen up the race. I knew that Bjorn Leukemans or he was going to try something because I was faster at the sprint. They were nervous, the guys from Vacansoleil! In the last bump, Leukemans had attacked, I had anticipated his move and I threw myself into his wheel. I led him, because we get on well together. When you're in a breakaway group with him, it's always a good sign. He wanted to win, he really made me feel it and he even asked me for it! Me, I didn't want to do too much either, to leave on my own and play the smart ass. Do you know why? Because I had looked at the images of the E3 Grand Prix again. I'm certain that if Cancellara had not exposed himself in that way on that day by wanting to do a solo number, he would not have been so entangled in the tactical marking in Flanders and Roubaix. With Leukemans, I said that victory was played with the pedal, no deal was possible. I had three reasons for winning: the prestige, I told him, of a race with an interesting record; the presence of Mark Frederix, who lives in Overijse and works with the National Lottery where he has always been exemplary where I was concerned, and then to prove to my team mates and my staff that I was ready for the Amstel Gold Race. Asking the others to work without bringing them anything is never a good idea.'

Phil imposed himself very easily in his duel with his friend Leukemans and for the second year running, it was a... Walloon who imposed himself in Overijse, twelve months after Sebastien Rosseler's unexpected success. While Phil received an ovation from the local public and from the many supporters from his fan club who had made the trip, a rumour was circulating in the wings: the probable separation of Omega Pharma and Lotto at the end of the season. *'I had heard talk of it but it wasn't my problem. I'm in a crucial phase, I don't want to lose focus on account of that',* he said before the journalists in a schoolyard next to the arrival. *When I returned to the hotel, I read my texts, I obviously receive quite a few but I can't answer everyone immediately and all the time. On the other hand, there was one that caught my attention immediately, from Davide Rebellin. He said: "The Brabant Arrow isn't part of the triple but it's beautiful nevertheless. Well done, keep going !"* In fact, without our knowing it, this Arrow had served as an aperitif for the copious repast that was awaiting us.

CHAPTER 10

The Amstel Gold Race - Absolute Perfection

Even though, at Overijse, he hadn't made a show like Cancellera's in the 3E Grand Prix, Philippe knew better than anyone that he would leave, on Sunday, not only wearing the number one but also with the enormous placard of favourite to defend his title in the Amstel Gold Race. *'The Nr 1 race bib has often been good for me: with it, I won the Paris-Tours, the Tour of Piedmont and the Tour of Lombardy - not bad, eh?'* He was also to win, in September, the Grand Prix of Quebec, because, to thank him for having come from across the Atlantic, the organizers had given him the Nr I race bib.

On the day after his victory in Overijse, an important piece of information was disseminated via the press: Cadel Evans had announced that he was withdrawing from the Ardennes classics, ill recovered from an injury to his quadriceps following a fall during training on 31 March. It didn't seem much, but it meant one less contender. *'However, I'm in a period of pomp, it's difficult to explain and it could be seen as pretention but at a couple of days before the Amstel, I'm sure of myself, and of my team: it's a pretty good feeling to share. But all the same, you can't say to anybody that nothing can happen to you! Especially as I am not a tooth-and-nail defender of the Amstel Gold Race and its organisation. Narrow roads, cars parked anywhere, undisciplined people, it's a dangerous race where a fall is always on the cards.'*

The NH Hotel, A Lucky Charm?

Under the sun, still and always, of a summer before its time, Philippe is resting in a quiet district of Maastricht, beside the Palace of the Congresses. The NH Hotel, he didn't know it yet, was going to bring him luck. Inside, between the bar and the reception, the owner furthermore had put some celebrity jerseys on display on the walls. The place breathes cycling and a passion for it: it's important for the cyclists, so cherished and protected. In the gently sloping little garden that borders the side entrance, Alan was playing with his father under the tender eyes of Patricia and his family. *'Patricia is from the area, she's taking advantage of it to see her parents and her family again, and then, by staying in the Netherlands, I'm less bothered than in Liege, for example. I need a maximum of concentration and rest. The life of the cyclist, when he isn't racing, is one of saving energy, of avoiding stairs, and overly long walks. As of my arrival, I was welcomed with Champagne, the owner wanted to congratulate me on my victory in Overijse. On Friday, we reccied the last 60 kilometres, but there were no surprises. I explained to the younger ones where and how they should place themselves, that their nervous system would be put to the test in a race where all the pitfalls are joined together. I also note that Jürgen Van den Broeck and Jelle Vanendert are well honed: they have done some good work. We're ready; I just have to face the press on Friday afternoon.'*

The 'Cancellara of the Ardennes'

The Dutch television channel (NOS), which had called Gilbert the 'Cancellara of the Ardennes' in its previous day's news bulletin, had installed its cameras in the basement of the NH Hotel. There were many more journalists there than usual. Marc Sergeant started by mentioning the dismissal of the Australian Matthew Lloyd from the Omega Pharma-Lotto team for behaviour that had brought cycling into disrepute but which had nothing to do with doping. The information didn't seem to interest the journalists, impatient to know all about the state of mind of the big favourite, to whom a first colleague evidently asked whether he wasn't afraid of being a victim of an anti-race like Cancellara.

> *'No! And then have you seen his prize list since San Remo? He has had three out of three of the first monumental podiums, and that, few riders can do. Then, you can't race defensively in races like the Amstel or Liege. Even if I'm marked to the seat of my pants, even if certain teams want to isolate me, they would nevertheless have to release me on the bumps.'*

The previous year, before imposing himself on the top of the Cauberg, Philippe had attacked earlier in the race, had exposed himself already, taking the risk perhaps, of no longer being to do a spurt on arrival. What was he going to do this time?

'Like in the Brabant Arrow: that would be ideal. There, I attacked once to make up the gap on the breakaway group. Afterwards, I let it happen. If I could find myself in similar conditions on Sunday, it would be perfect. If my team is in top form as I hope it will be, I can wait for the final ascent. Jurgen Van den Broeck and Jelle Vanendert have assured me of their support and I know that, except for a mishap, they will be in the final group. I'm not afraid of anybody in particular but rather of teams, of coalitions. The Katusha team looks the best on paper, with Rodriguez but also Ivanov, who has already won here. The Rabobank team is playing at home in front of Gesink's supporters; there will also be many Luxembourg fans for the Schleck brothers. There will be lots of people: it's a World Tour race which I know by heart. When I was still living in Belgium, in the winter I would regularly come to this neck of the woods because it has a microclimate that means that it can easily be five degrees warmer than in the Ardennes.'

'If I win, I'll take Alan on to the podium'

A little cycling on the Saturday, some rest, and meetings with close relations. Everything is calm and serene, while on the Maastricht Town Square there's permanent effervescence, tactical discussions between the sports managers at the time of the organisation's briefing, the immutable five o'clock meeting on the eve of a big race. *'I have something in mind: if I win, I'll take the infant on to the podium. I want Alan to be the youngest Gilbert of all time to have mounted a podium. Me, I had had to wait for a provincial championship in 1997 to savour that particular pleasure!'*

In Maastricht, on the Sunday morning, the weather was so clement that coffee was being served on the terraces at eight o'clock in the morning! Gaily dressed in orange and with flags vaunting the merits of their beer, the Dutch were impatient to see their new god, Robert Gesink, the winner of the Tour of Oman, who had marked the Amstel in red letters in his notebook. He was not the only one, in the Rabobank team, where the inescapable Oscar Freire also had something in mind. The Omega Pharma-Lotto bus, for its part, was practically inaccessible, as was that of the Leopards, invaded by an impressive colony of Andy and Frank Schleck fans. Slightly back from this crowd, imbued by its certainty and its desires, Marc Sergeant was conversing about cabbages and kings with his usual lofty views. And he even dared to say, which was not like him: *'If we don't have a technical hitch or a fall, I think that Phil is unbeatable.'*

What confidence ! *'Perhaps I had communicated it to the entire team? Could be. In any case, the guys have worked well before the appointment. I see them and I know that they're all focused. Behind the breakaway group, already, they were on the job but without overdoing it. At 90 kilometres from the arrival, the Rabobanks decided to toughen up the race; they gave us a fabulous helping hand because that unbridled the race, there were distinctly fewer riders at the back. We patiently waited without unnecessarily coming out behind the attempts of Tankink, Barredo or Luis-Leon Sanchez. Those three were working either for Gesink, or for Freire: in any event, I had to keep an eye on them.'*

In front, the Rabobanks were starting however to feel that if they overdid it, they wouldn't have any more juice for finishing the job. The Leopard team furthermore fairly quickly took over by ensuring a high tempo before Frank Schleck and Fabian Cancellara fell, on a straight piece of road, in the middle of the group. This fall disrupted the Leopards' plans and it was accompanied by the Katushas, mainly, that the Omega Pharmas set up shop in the avant-garde of the peloton.

'I'm the most complete racer'

'On the three hills in the final stretch before the Cauberg, Van den Broeck and Vanendert ensured such a pace that it would have complicated anyone's attack. Rodriguez (Katusha) had had a good try on the Keutenberg but he had soon realised it was a waste of time and effort because I had told Jelle to ensure the same tempo. Even before the top, we had caught the Spaniard. I was comple-

tely at ease, I hadn't yet had to get involved in this race, and that changed me
a little! And then, above, Andy Schleck left on the dip. Protected by Fulgsang
at the head of the peloton, he could try. There again I didn't panic even though
when I had gone to see the Rabobanks and the Katushas, nobody had wanted
to take over. So I did the work with Jürgen and Jelle. When the game became
more technical at five kilometres from the arrival, I benefited from the descent to
put myself at the head of the group, too bad if nobody took over from me. I was
regularly doing 65 kph on the winding parts where Andy couldn't decently go
more quickly than me. With the television channel's motorbike, furthermore, I
had him practically all the time in my sights. I wanted to delay the joining up
for as long as possible so that the others wouldn't benefit from it. The gap never
climbed above twenty seconds and when we arrived at the foot of the Cauberg,
what a beautiful surprise when I saw Jelle arriving! He had come from the back
and as nobody had taken over from me for a while, his helping hand did me a
power of good. Above all, it broke the others' morale. The Rabobanks and the
Katushas had thought that they had had me thanks to their collective presence,
but they were wrong. Because my morale, at that moment, was sky-high. I had
at first let Rodriguez go, who had overtaken Andy, but he was in too high a
gear, and I could easily see that he was at his maximum. I looked back to see
whether others were reacting but they were cooked, so I then I accelerated and
swept past Rodriguez. I also benefited from those hectometres of madness, where
I had the impression of being with the Standard de Liege football team. There
was shouting everywhere. I looked on both sides of the road where people were
waving, then when I passed in front of the podium, I looked for Patricia and
Alan, but I didn't see them, there were too many people. Close to my trainer, I
first wanted to breathe, in fact, I was feeling a lot of emotion. I very quickly had
the feeling of having ridden a perfect race, something I dream about but cannot
always control, on the same scale as my second victory in the Tour of Lombardy.
I remember saying at the press conference that I felt that I was the most complete
racer for one-day races. That was perhaps pretentious of me but on reflection,
given the previous podiums in San Remo or the Tour of Flanders, was I completely wrong?'

Not at all, because apart from Contador and Evans, absolutely nobody was
missing. The nobs of world cycling were united in their raptures about Phil's
performance, acclaimed as ever by his partisans assembled for several hours

beyond the line in front of a giant screen and fortunately supplied with cold drinks, those of the local sponsor in particular, because they were really needed for lubricating the emotions that had been so long contained. On the podium, Alan Gilbert made his appearance under the acclamations of the delirious crowd. The voice of the announcer who was shouting in his ear finally exasperated him, and with a scream which the man with the microphone will remember for a long time, Alan let him know that he had heard enough of him ! The emotion, the stress and all the hullabaloo was too much for the infant, quickly recovered by his mum.

In the profusion of the comments distilled after the race, that of Eddy Merckx was worthy of special attention. *Philippe is at the top of his art, but so is his team. If it rides like that in Liege, he will win, that's for sure.*

Many indeed have saluted the collective performance of the Omega Pharma-Lotto team, the symbiosis around Gilbert, the calm and the tactical control of an often criticized unit. *'I've never managed a racer like him',* was to be said later by Marc Sergeant who never put himself forward to assert any particular tactical hold on the race. *'The riders did all the work, to perfection, I would say. It's so rare for a sports manager to see that.'* However, it was only a... beginning. Even if there was an intense focus, already, on the next objective when, on getting to Maastricht beyond the incredible traffic jams, the cyclists of the Belgian team were sipping the champagne offered, of course, by the management of the NH Hotel. Which was becoming a lucky charm for Philippe. *'This Champagne was well deserved, because the protocol had been extremely long. The anti-doping, the press conferences, all those people who want to touch you, to get an autograph: I was in a hurry to get some peace and quiet, to savour the moment, to see the images again...'*

CHAPTER 11

The Wall of Huy, a Football Stadium

At the NH Hotel, the wine waiter was once again busy uncorking bottles of Champagne on the evening of the triumph in Valkenburg. Within the intimacy of the team, it was party time, because everybody was conscious, beyond Philippe's performance, that the Omega Pharma-Lotto team had been up to it. Marc Sergeant, a fine connoisseur, had preferred to savour a 'triple Affligem', the beer of his native land. *'If we remain this focused, if we apply ourselves like this around Philippe in Liege, failing a catastrophe, victory will open its arms to Gilbert. I know that he really wants it, and so do we!'*

Curiously, nobody mentioned the Walloon Arrow, which was however taking place on the following Wednesday. Just right, it was said in the Belgian team's camp, for it to be an opportunity for Van den Broeck or Vanendert to play a personal card. Philippe, for his part, had received a very explicit text from Davide Rebellin: *'So that's one with the Amstel: you still have two to go, but I have no doubt about it.'*

'My Wheelie goes wrong at the hotel: a moment of shame!'

When I went to bed on the Sunday evening, I decided that I had to turn the page, forget the Amstel, have some rest, and get my feet back on the ground as quickly as possible. In my mind, in relation to my objectives, I was nowhere. I had reached a stage, confirmed that I had a hand in that kind of arrival, and a good team around me. No excess, and above all, no euphoria. I didn't want any and I endeavoured to ensure that this mindset would be the watchword for everyone.

On Monday, when returning from training, I made THE blunder of the season, which could have cost me dear. When I arrived at the lawn by the hotel, I played with my bicycle as I always do by finishing my number with a Wheelie (raising the front wheel and maintaining balance for as long as possible while riding, an exercise that mountain bikers practise on a regular basis). The problem was that I had underestimated the steepness of the slope near the hotel's embankment and I went backwards in splendid sunlight that would have delighted the photographers or the cameras. I had never told anyone that, as you might well imagine, because I was little ashamed! I had injured my elbow, and had hurt the small of my back. I was furious with myself; I flagellated myself, calling myself a real beginner, an idiot, a kid. The osteopath treated me that evening but, on the Tuesday morning, my back was still aching. Just think, on the eve of the Arrow! My elbow was bandaged but, at the press conference, nobody asked me why, and it wasn't terribly noticeable either, and then I didn't want to talk about it!'

Facing the press, Philippe minimised his chances of winning the Walloon Arrow. *'The Wall of Huy* (where nevertheless he came 6th in 2010, 11 seconds behind Evans), *is too hard for me, too steep, it's really a thing for the pure climbers. Unless I can anticipate by leaving from further away. In recent years, everything has been played for on the last ascent because the weather was too good, because there hadn't been a race beforehand. The race will not in any event weigh us down. We have won the Amstel Gold Race, the other teams know that they don't have many more opportunities for winning; it's for them to assume their responsibilities. Sincerely, in my mind, I regard the Arrow as my best training before the "Doyenne".'*

For the specialists who have been following Philippe's exploits since the beginning of the season, what he said was seen as a dexterous way of diverting people's attention. Double winner of the Walloon Arrow, Claude Criquielion said this in an interview with 'Le Soir': *'The stage that Philippe won in Tirreno with Evans, Scarponi, Cunego and company among the adversaries, that was largely worth the intensity and the difficulty of the Arrow. Furthermore, he has nothing to lose, he has no pressure, and he's on exceptional form. In his place, I would take advantage of it because he will perhaps never again have an opportunity to turn up at the start under such optimal conditions'.* Same remarks from Rik Verbrugghe, the last Walloon winner in Huy ten years earlier and Gilbert's future sports manager at BMC. *'Phil knows the course by heart: his team is ready. For us (BMC), he's once again the one to beat. It's out of the question to wait for the foot of the final ascent since we don't have Cadel Evans, forfeited. For a lad like Van Avermaet, for example, anticipation is essential. For Philippe, it was too. I'm speaking in the past tense because, as he is in the zone, and even with the climbers, I can't see who can beat him.'*

At the Charleroi start, in any case, there was no clapometer photograph. The papers were united in suggesting to Philippe that he shouldn't snub the Arrow.

'I hadn't the slightest intention of snubbing it ! I wanted in the back of my mind to win it but it was complicated and that was confirmed at the start. After the first 80 kilometres, I wasn't great. Fortunately, there was a big breakaway group in front, even though it contained none of ours. I had admittedly explained at the briefing that we would decide our action plan starting from the second ascent of the Wall of Huy, there were limits all the same ! I rallied the troops via the earpiece. I even shouted: "Come on, lads. Let's race !" We had an enormous advantage since the beginning of the race: the same teams were ensuring the pursuit, sometimes the Saxo Banks for Contador, sometimes the Leopards for the Schleck brothers. When all those lovely people saw us reapplying with Van den Broeck and Vanendert, there were looks that spoke volumes. I was blocked. Around fiftieth place at the time of the second Wall and, frankly, I was feeling better and better. It's true that the race wasn't moving, a hundred of us had arrived at the foot for a mind-blowing sprint. I use this expression because you need to be in the Arrow's peloton to understand. It's a game of elbows, while some push the others with their knees or even hit their wheels. It's not seen on television but that's what happens inside !'

'My communion with the public'

On the ascent of the Chemin des Chapelles, the crazy street that leads to the Huy tennis club and the Sarte recreation ground, a kind of insanity gripped the public, massed as ever on the steep embankments that serve as vantage points for the spectators. The heat was already stifling, and it was even more so when they waved flags and jerseys. All that was needed was a trio of referees to add to the atmosphere of a football match. The spectators reckoned on the second passage that Phil could win the Arrow. His face conveyed the serenity of the strong, like that of a boxer sure of himself at the approach of the final round.

'We were all of course at the mercy of a winning attack. The more so as when I got to the front, the other teams were riding less strongly. When Pineau (Quick Step) left with Marcato (Vacansoleil), it was dangerous nevertheless. I had even thought of counter-attacking with Vinokourov but the peloton was going too fast. But Jurgen Van den Broeck did some phenomenal work on the plain to reduce the gap and, me, I was wedged between the wheels of the Rabobanks. I'm not certain of having pedalled too much before the last 1,500 metres! I sincerely hadn't prepared anything, I felt good, but all the favourites were there. Instinctively, I glanced at the faces of Contador, the Schleck brothers and Rodriguez: they were fairly badly placed at the approach of the famous "S" where the adversaries should be pushed inwards in order to make them take the most difficult gradient. I gained 10% by that glance. Instinctively, I had accelerated when I was at the wheels of Christophe Mevel, and then I had cut my trajectory, which nonplussed my rivals for a moment. I knew that Rodriguez had counter-attacked but I was carried by the public. I had mentioned a Standard Liege football match atmosphere in the Amstel, but here, it was even louder, because the ascent of the Wall is narrow, and the people can practically touch you. I was flying. My brother who was at the 200-metre panel told me later that behind me, when the other riders had passed, there was a cathedral-like silence. I was frightened of being caught, as in Tirreno where Scarponi and Evans had hurt me but when I realised that I had *made the decisive gap, I measured my strength, my state of grace, the fact that never, in my career, had I climbed the Chemin des Chapelles so quickly even if, during the last 100 metres, I was doing 2 km per hour because I wanted to communicate with the public, share a moment that I will perhaps live never again.'*

'I reckon that what is happening to me is enormous, that thousands of people were expecting it, that they screamed their joy and their relief. My whole family was there: there was an exceptional atmosphere.'

'You see kid, you've done it!'

Between the public and its hero carried on to the podium like a boxer receiving his belt, the paroxysm of the joy was reached under the admiring eyes of Bernard Hinault, five-time winner of the Tour who was responsible for the protocol for the Amaury Sport Organisation, organizer of the Arrow and the Liege-Bastogne-Liege. *'You see kid, you've done it: there was no reason to fear the gradient of the Wall. Cash in, cash in: when you're on such form, you should jump on everything that moves.'* The Breton didn't realise how right he was.

'When I was young, the Arrow was a monument, a dream Wednesday with my parents, especially because the race at that time started from Spa, so it was easier for us to go to see the riders. Hinault was right: the more I won, the more confident I felt, the more I wanted to win. It's a kind of euphoria that I reckon is ephemeral. In this spiral, the others look at you as though you're an extraterrestrial: their morale is rock bottom. I know that I'm lucky, that I'm on the form of my life. I almost know for sure that I will also pull off that treble that Davide Rebellin had mentioned. I know finally that the comments are tinged with jealousy, that doubts are arising and that some are saying: "But what's he on?" When I say that I'm lucky, I'll extend the analysis further: the climate is magnificent, rare in April for an Arrow; the adversaries are not on top form, I've already seen Contador better than that. I'll end up by making Rodriguez sick: he's always second. I think of all that when I get off my bike again, after all my post-protocol obligations, to get back into to the bus. People were still waiting for me but I gave a minimum of autographs. There again, I wanted to run away, to

cocoon myself in my concentration to the best of my ability, like in a religious retreat. Especially not to hear it said, at a later date: "A bit greedy, that Gilbert, if
he doesn't win the Doyenne, he'll know why!" Even if I hadn't won the Arrow,
I would have still been one of the big favourites for the Liege-Bastogne-Liege;
it didn't change anything for me.' In the Huy Tennis Club that served as the
press room that day, a journalist asked a question to which the answer was to
make the Thursday morning's media headlines: 'Can you tell us where your
limits now are?'

'The Eiffel Tower on the Easter cake'

'My limits? To be honest, I no longer know myself where they are!
Previously, they were to do with imposing myself on my dream events:
the Milan-San Remo, the Tour of Lombardy, the Liege, the Walloon
Arrow, I didn't think that the possibility existed. As much to say that
it gives me enormous confidence for the future: perhaps other races
that I hadn't believed in will henceforth be part of my concerns.' In
his euphoria, Phil kept a noble heart. 'I finished my press conference
by dedicating my bouquet to François Vanassche, a great man in the
service of cycling in Wallonia. I am certain that this victory would
have brought him a lot of joy, and his father Yves, who was on the
finishing line. I have thought of him with emotion: this success is also
his.'

In the furnace of the improvised VIP lounges, on both sides of the finishing
line, the guests were gobsmacked by Gilbert's demonstration. Eddy Merckx,
the greatest VIP of them all, declared: 'I'm full of admiration, and above all
impressed. I have got to know the man, recently, and have fallen under his spell.
What he's achieving for the moment is better than Merckx! I've liked his way
of managing the competition. In the Amstel, he assumed the pursuit himself
behind Andy Schleck before attacking. Here, he did the opposite, but it was
more impressive because nothing was in his favour: there were too many people
at the foot of the final ascent, the lighter builds were already counting their
chickens, and then he left at 400 metres without opposition. He had waited for
the best moment, it's easy to say so afterwards, but, in cycling, choosing the right

moment isn't simple, it's an art. If one had to race only with ones legs, many people would have won a multitude of races. Gilbert also rides with his head. He will win in Liege: then it will no longer be a cherry but the Eiffel Tower on the Easter cake!'

If Eddy says so...

970396Y MTCARL F
117 1327
250500CC PARIS F

ZCZC YCC180 IGF505 GRV700 TLX-0049 BE11042700131
MCMX CO BEBR 082
BRUXELLES/BRUSSEL 082/072 27 1308

A MONSIEUR PHILIPPE GILBERT

COMME UNE MULTITUDE DE BELGES,NOUS AVONS SUIVI AVEC FIERTE VOTRE
MAGNIFIQUE PERFORMANCE A LA DOYENNE. LIEGE-BASTOGNE-LIEGE. 2011.
NOUS VOUS FELICITONS DE TOUT COEUR POUR VOTRE PALMARES EXCEPTIONNEL
DE CES DIX DERNIERS JOURS AVEC QUATRE VICTOIRES SUCCESSIVES
(LA FLECHE BRABANCONNE, L'AMSTEL GOLD RACE, LA FLECHE WALLONNE
ET LIEGE - BASTOGNE-LIEGE)ET VOUS SOUHAITONS ENCORE BEAUCOUP DE
SUCCES LORS DES COMPETITIONS A VENIR.
        ALBERT ET PAOLA

NNNN
970396Y MTCARL F
250500CC PARIS F

CHAPTER 12

A Holy Week

Davide Rebellin's prediction was coming true, step by step, in something of a frenzied atmosphere. If it had been excited about him before, Belgium was finally assessing Philippe Gilbert as not only an excellent racer in the classics but also the best in the world in that discipline. On the Thursday morning, he was unofficially the world number one (unofficially because the ranking appeared on the following Monday). In the furnace of a summer spring, after having struck camp at the Wall of Huy, the organizers moved to Ans, like a merry-go-round moving from fair to fair. The enthusiasm was already palpable as of the Thursday, three days before the Liege-Bastogne-Liege. Never had it reached such a paroxysm, especially in Remouchamps, where the 'Fan Club' was busy setting up its annual festivities on the Redoute hillside. An immense marquis was erected on it, and the fun started inside it as of the Friday, sportive or dancing according to individual mood. A French reporter tasked with conveying the atmosphere exclaimed: *'I've never seen anything like it in my life before a cycle race.'* Lower down, in the valley, the village had dressed itself up as Gilbert, in his team's colours, the bistro-owners were organised, the pirate barbecues were waiting for sausages, while on the tarmac of the famous Ardennes hills, the paint pot merchants were doing a roaring trade: 'PHIL' was to be seen painted everywhere, even on the trees!

'I'm in my bubble'

At the training, the riders were impressed by all the preparations. On the Redoute, on the famous left turn that starts the steepest rise of the famous Remouchamps headland, the first camping cars were already there. *'First come, first served!'*, a Termonde pensioner guffawed.

In his Dutch NH Hotel retreat, Philippe was preparing for what he had always hitherto considered to be the race of his year, the race of his life perhaps, the one which, sentimentally, connected him to the umbilical faith that he had maintained since his first cycling hours on earth.

'I know that there's a lot happening around me, I can guess, I can imagine the intensity of the preparations in Remouchamps, but I'm withdrawn from the world. I habitually answer the texts or the e-mails from faithful friends who send me their words of encouragement or congratulations, but even for them, I have to restrain myself. On Wednesday evening, some members of the fan club had come to Maastricht: they knew that it was easier to see me, as I had taken advantage of it to give my winner's bouquet to my mother. To save time, I had had my shower in the bus because I had been warned that I was going out live in the evening news bulletin. Afterwards, I watched the images, with Jelle Vanendert, of the Amstel and the Arrow. It's always interesting to see the final sprints because I can quickly detect what was good or less good, the tactics of the adversaries, and their form too. Even if it was of course perfect with two victories, I'm a perfectionist; I identify anything that was not OK.'

'I'm in a bubble. As far as the requests from the press were concerned, Omega Pharma-Lotto had organised real barrage, which had been essential. A single press conference for everyone on the Friday, if not, it was impossible. I had applied the same instructions for the training. It's true, I know the roads of Liège-Bastogne-Liège by heart but not inevitably the state of the roads, which deteriorate from one winter to another, but I knew that they had suffered more than usual in recent months and I saw it with my own eyes: what a catastrophe! So we made a little reccy, but not starting from Wanne like most of them, but simply from the Maquisard hill at Spa. That was some 60 kilometres. The team bus was waiting for us on our arrival at the Ans car park, where there were some supporters, as well as an RTBF team, but I politely refused to be interviewed, I preferred to concentrate that obligation into the one and only press conference.'

Around the NH Hotel, on the Friday, the car parks were not sufficient to accommodating the TV antennas, the media from everywhere, and the gawpers in search of an autograph, or a photograph. The early summer was still there, the heat was even stifling, as verified in the coal-black sky: a huge storm was threatening. In the conference room in the basement, there was no more room for any latecomer journalists. The timing was tight but Phil applied himself, as usual, in all the languages that he speaks, among which Italian for an interview for the *RAI*.

'I wasn't happy with my Friday's training. Paradoxically, I had better legs on Thursday, on the day after the Arrow, but I think that everyone was a bit in the same boat. We're in a pretty heavy period: a lot of recovery is required. It was much better on Saturday. I had slept well the night before and rather than going back over the course, I remained in Maastricht and in its surroundings. I made my legs turn behind Dirk De Wolf's car for a good hour, pushing the needle up to 85 kph at times. That enabled me to check that my speeds were finally OK! In that exercise behind the car, I felt that I had legs of fire and when that happens, I just pray that it will be same next day! To the Press, I explained that, like each time, I had put the dials back to zero, as if I hadn't won anything. It's the only manner of proceeding. I attach no importance to the comments, the eulogies or the thanks, I concentrate, I get myself massaged, I eat correctly, and I leave nothing to chance.'

In the pre-race discussions, among the interviews conducted here and there, many mentioned Frank Vandenbroucke's victory in 1999 and therefore the last by a Belgian rider, but what a one! On that day too there had been fire on the lanes that meander between the pastures. The Belgians, largely dominated thereafter by the likes of Rebellin, Bettini and Valverde, had practically not been allowed to say another word. On the other hand, right from his first appearance in the peloton, Philippe had set himself a medium-term objective, a major obsession, and his progress was conveyed each year by some increasingly convincing results. As if it were necessary to tame this 'Doyenne' with considerable tact, Phil did not get ahead of himself. On the other hand, this time, he was found more than ever in the shoes of the mega-favourite, the man against whom you should certainly not bet on the bookies' websites.

'I'll never say, as Frank Vandenbroucke did in 1999, that I'm sure of winning: for me, that's the best way of losing. But it's pretty special to experience a week like this one. To win Liege would be fabulous, but I've never managed to. In 2009, I wasn't 100%, I had no choice but to attack early, on the Hill of Hornay at Sprimont before being caught by Andy Schleck in La Roche-aux-Faucons. And last year, it was on that same hill that I lost after counter-attacking behind the attackers.'

'The most beautiful race in the world'

Even if he kept his charisma, a disarming calm in front of the Press, Phil let himself go, his heart spoke when he admitted: 'Liege is longer, harder, it's the most beautiful race in the world, in any case for me. You have to deserve it, I want it a lot, that's clear. I would happily exchange all the races that I've won up to now against the Liege-Bastogne-Liege because, when I was a kid, I used to watch the champions on La Redoute, and when I became a young rider, I already reckoned that it was the most beautiful. I would like to benefit from the atmosphere, and the public, as I was able to at the Arrow: that would be great. I know that I'm expected to win by thousands of supporters: that does something to me, but I prefer not to think of it right now. When you have your head down towards the tarmac where your Christian name is written in big letters at every metre, that does something, I'm moved by it each time.'

In his concern for perfection, Phil had also discovered, in 2010, that the team games had been unfavourable to him. He had had to ride against pairs and, eventually, it was no longer possible to react behind everyone, which had benefitted Vinokourov and Kolobnev.

'Last summer, I discussed the preparation for the spring of 2011 a lot with the guys. All of us have now been preoccupied for six months for this week that I hold so dear. Each has trained and worked hard to get to this point, to help me to achieve my goals. That has worked well up to now and I thank them. Now the job has to be done !

*In addition to Van den Broeck, I have Vanendert and Bakelants,
in particular, who can hope to be there in the final sprint. That's
very important for me. Because I'm not afraid of any adversary in
particular but of alliances: Rodriguez with Kolobnev, the Schleck
brothers, Samuel Sanchez and then Vinokourov, who is very strong.
He has the advantage of having already won the Doyenne twice: it's
an argument in his favour. Andy is good as well. He worked for his
brother in the Arrow but I reckon his legs are already in good shape.'*

Phil already had the race in his mind: his procedure, his tactical planning.
He added, there again, in a statement different from that which he usually
makes when a journalist asks him whether he would be disappointed in the
event of defeat. *'Extremely, especially if I'm second or third. I'm the favourite
but I'm not Eddy Merckx. I don't win with a two-minute lead on my adversaries, that's impossible. Look at Rodriguez; he was there each time, not far from
everything, both in the Amstel and in the Arrow. If everyone races against me
like the others did against Cancellara in the Paris-Roubaix, all the favourites
will be beaten ! If my competitors want to have a chance of winning, they must
take me along with them, especially in a race as selective as the Liege. The ideal
scenario would be a fight at 7 or 8, man against man at the end, in order to
judge who is the best. I have the advantage, in such a situation, of having a
sprint. That's my trump card.'*

In the intimacy of his date with himself, when he's not in discussions with
his team mates or the sports managers, Phil is conscious of having a date
with history. *'I've taken care of all the details, I'm ready - mentally and physically. The day before, I ate a steak that I had asked to be perfect. I fell peacefully
asleep at around 11 p.m. and when I closed my eyes, I knew that it was going to
be OK.'*

Marc Sergeant, his placid sports manager, shared that serenity. Better, he
maintained it. *'Philippe has had an exceptionally successful spring but I know
that he'll only be happy if he wins the Liege-Bastogne-Liege. After that, nothing
can happen to him, except bad luck. I dream of seeing him contest the victory
with Rodriguez in a duel in Ans: that would be coherent in the light of what
we've seen so far.'*

CHAPTER 13

My Date with the 'Doyenne'

The sky was already blue when the sun broke through in Maastricht. It was a good sign: there would not be a Dantean version like that of 1980 when Bernard Hinault had finished with frozen fingers on the Boulevard de la Sauvenière.

'I had a good long shower. Dirk Leenaert had slipped me the notion that my legs were bombs after having massaged them the previous day. I took good note of it! At breakfast, I'm often one of the last to leave the table. I take the time to eat slowly: it's crucial before a long classic. On the other hand, we arrived far too early at the Place Saint-Lambert start. We were afraid that there might be traffic jams and Marc Sergeant had logically wanted to make allowances. When you're already dressed, in battle dress, and you have to wait for an hour and a half in the bus, it's very long. There, I get a little stressed. The televised interviews before the races irritate me as well. What more can I bring a quarter of an hour before the start? Nothing, if not to repeat what I had said the day before. When I went to sign the competitor sheet, there was an impressive guard of honour. The encouragements did me good: I was focused but completely relaxed. I knew that I had a date with La Doyenne.'

Madness on La Redoute

On that Easter Sunday, the belfries were resounding to their heart's content, much to the liking of the villages that irremediably lead to the tops of the Ardennes in that interminable advance through the enormous fir trees that dominate the hill of the Baraque de Fraiture. From the motorway which leads to the top of the Belgian Ardennes, one could see, already, the massed crowd on La Redoute - many hours before the riders' passage. All hands on deck, Philippe's parents and his entire family were doing the 'catering' in an overheated marquis *'I've so much to do that I can't even see the screen or what what's happening in the race,'* puffed his mother, Anita. Lower down, in the centre of Remouchamps, one could see even more animation at the 'Cheval Blanc', at Dédé's, a supporter from the very beginning who, at each of Philippe's victories, adds a figure on the front of his establishment. The places were expensive: people were in the middle of the road to see the first passage in their hero's birthplace.

> *'For me, it's a bad memory! Because the race had started flat out, like all the classics up to that point furthermore, and I had warned everyone that they had to be attentive. Instead of that, we had no-one in the morning breakaway group, and that annoyed me. I was "bellowing" into the earpieces, so I hardly had time to appreciate the applause in my village. Then a man had got through a phenomenal amount of work that day that was to count, later, in the race: Jurgen Van de Walle had been mind-blowing at the head of the peloton. Without him, the race would perhaps have been lost. But my worries weren't over. Later, in the Wanne-Stockeu-Haute Levée trilogy, Van den Broeck, especially, was badly placed. On the Stavelot dip after the Haute-Levée, I even found myself all on my own. But I had legs of fire. If I had no more team mates, perhaps it was because they were unwell? I never panicked. Fortunately, I found the guys a little later and Van den Broeck, who had admitted to me that it wasn't his day, had sacrificed himself on the Maquisard and then on the Mont-Theux to ensure the pace behind the breakaway group. The goal was to take me to the foot of La Redoute under the best conditions.'*

In front, it was always the same scenario except that a counter-attack group had caught the first breakaways. There were nevertheless some fine players with Van Avermaet, Gasparotto, Pineau, Garate and Ten Dam, but still no Omega Pharma-Lotto. But no Leopard either. The Belgian team found a weighty ally with the Luxembourg formation and that was verified on La Redoute, where Monfort, Fulgsang and company eclipsed the Schleck brothers.

'Me, I was protected by Jelle, while having goose pimples when we were approaching Remouchamps. It's always very special in a race, especially this one. I know each house, the people who live there; I ride past my sister's home, and past that of my parents. Then the most solemn moment, for me, is without doubt when I ride close to the cemetery where my grandparents are buried. It's just before going up the road towards La Redoute. I knew that I was alone in the peloton, and at that precise moment, I felt an emotion that I cannot share. On La Redoute, it was weird. I had the feeling of ascending a pass in the Tour de France through people. I had seldom been carried like that by the public: I had the feeling that the people were pedalling for me. At that particular moment, I was extremely serene; I even dare to admit it: I was certain that I was going to win. The breakaway group didn't have much of a lead, we had stabilised behind it, and the Leopards were riding with us because the Schleck brothers wanted to win and they were OK.'*

Frank Schleck: 'We're going to the end and the three of us will fight it out'

The weather was clement, and despite the sustained rhythm, there were still some fine players at the end. At the foot of La Roche-aux-Faucons, that new hill that has served twice as arbiter in previous years, Van Avermaet (BMC) and Gasparotto (Astana) seemed the freshest of the survivors. Behind, it was Andy Schleck who was catching fire.

'I didn't stand up on my pedals to follow him: that was an enormous sign for me. Frank had taken over immediately and me too, which had enabled the three of us to be together fairly quickly. Behind, Jelle Vanendert had left the hole without moving, and he played an active role in the final break. On this subject, Vinokourov told me afterwards: "He did his work so well that, on the subject of breaking, he broke my wheel as well!" It's true, Jelle and Vino had collided and my friend Alex had lost the race there, whereas he could have been in the game. In front, I never prevaricated. Even if I was

*jammed between the two brothers, Frank came level with me and
told me: "We'll race flat out and we'll have a three-way fight at the
end." I greatly appreciated that sportsmanship, that class in relation
to the event. As though you always reap what you sow. Remember
what I said about Cancellara in the Tour of Flanders: I have never
raced against him, but with him. Here, I know that everyone is
at my wheel, but, at least, there are now only two of them.' Three,
to be precise, because Van Avermaet didn't abdicate, he played the
windscreen-wiper role but one felt that at each difficulty, he was
paying for the waste of effort of his race, which was furthermore
magnificent.'*

Between the Luxemburg supporters and the local public, it was madness
because, as usual, Frank and Andy had displaced people. Without creating
a considerable gap on the pursuers who were trying to organise themselves
around Kreuziger and de Nibali, in particular, Philippe and the de Mondorf
brothers were in charge. They waited until Saint-Nicolas for the first fight. The
hill known as the 'Italians' was above all very Walloon that day, topped also by
the pretty Luxemburg flag perched on top of some enormous blue poles.

*'There was such serenity between us, and yet without any tacit
agreement, that neither Andy, Frank nor I were afraid of Van
Avermaet, who courageously returned each time. The ease with which
we had widened the gap in the La Roche-aux-Faucons served as
answers for what happened next. We knew that the fight would be
played out by the three of us. From the beginning in Saint-Nicolas,
Andy had set a very high tempo; I took over with a certain economy
because I was waiting for a really frank attack from Frank. Our
rhythm was so high (more than 500 watts, for those of you who are
in to statistics) that I knew that the surprise effect wouldn't be great.
On one of the most sloping bends, Frank put in his attack, but on
the outside of the bend! I just had to nip inside and, using much less
force than him, I find myself in front of him by saving two to three
metres by that trajectory. Then, I accelerated more and more to finish
by a mini sprint at practically 30kph at the top, which put me in my
dream situation, in a man-to-man combat. Because Andy had had*

*to let to us through before returning. I was even fresher than when I
had attacked Valverde in the previous year. I was watching them all
the time; I had dented their morale because they both understood,
as from beyond Saint-Nicolas, that they couldn't get me even if, in
theory, it was I who was jammed.'*

But we were not in the Rocourt tunnel where, in the past, the De Vlaeminck
brothers had jammed Eddy Merckx, safe from the watching eyes and the
cameras. On the Ans hill, three of the best riders in the world would be
fighting for the award of the last spring classic, and the most demanding one.
Supported by a whole population who had come, also, to save their jobs for
a few years in the local breweries, Philippe Gilbert was a few minutes from
his childhood dream. He saw the stars in the blinding sky of Rue Jean Jaurès,
but he didn't touch them. Not yet. The brothers were no longer attacking
him on the home straight. They were no longer able to. Frank had already
put his hands at the bottom of the handlebar: it was known that it would be
he who would try to oppose Philippe's sprint.

*'Those last two kilometres were the longest of my career. I was
impatient to do battle with them like a kid who is waiting for his ice
cream. They were titillating me. From the left-hand bend, I went on
the inside, I couldn't wait any longer and when the gap was made,
I was able reproduce my epic of the Arrow, and to benefit from it,
my favourite verb in the French language, and in every language
furthermore. I finally had that Doyenne, my conclusion of an historic,
and I now know, exceptional week. Perhaps it will never happen
again, I know that too. I would like in any case to pay homage to
Frank and Andy Schleck. We had obviously known each other for
a long time without having spoken much together. Their attitude,
without speculation, without calculation, without tactic dictated into
an earpiece, enabled a classic race to be seen. Finally, for me, it was
classic! I had great regard for their sporting attitude, it was elegant.
It's also called class, and it is not given to everyone.'*

Which the pair from the Grand Duchy, applauded by the entire crowd with
the same fervour as its local hero, was to confirm on the podium where, with

a noble gesture like a vassal before his lord, Frank made a low bow of admiration, which was worth all the speeches of the world.

'My Pink Champagne in Havelange'

In Ans, Remouchamps, and everywhere else, the television sets were red hot. The audiences had exploded; the barbecues had had a break, before starting again even better. It wasn't complicated: it was so hot that you just had to sigh on the embers for them to catch fire. The Schlecks fan club had practically requisitioned the bistro placed just opposite the podium since the beginning of the day. When the three cyclists mounted their podium, it was impossible to pass by on the pavements, even for a cigarette paper. Behind the scenes, Patricia was unable hold back her tears of joy and emotion. She, also, had dreamed of this moment, the one which she knew that her young husband would almost have preferred to her, for an ephemeral moment of euphoria that only top sportsmen and artists can reach. It is called 'grace', without any puns about Monaco where, there too, people were draped in pride. The infant Alan, as in Valkenburg, was taken up on to the podium where his father had dreamt of putting his feet since his tender childhood when he watched Bartali and company fighting it out in his village. Destiny had done its job. Some have said or written in the wake of such feats: 'Now, I can die', but that was not the case with Philippe.

In the Loncin sports hall, he announced furthermore, in the press room, what had been taken by many as a joke: *'Now, the yellow jersey'*. He wasn't speaking about the champion of Belgium jersey, but about the famous tunic of the Tour de France.

> *'I remember it perfectly. Brunhilde, our press executive, had had to control the situation because it was complicated with the media. Organising the sets for the TV cameras then for the written Press, with the antidoping controls in between, was not simple. Afterwards, we ate in an excellent Italian restaurant just a stone's throw from the arrival where I also gave a live interview in a TV news bulletin. But I was waiting for only one thing: to return to Remouchamps.*

I had promised my supporters that I would come, even if beaten.
Fortunately, my brother Christian had organised things as only he
knows how. A police escort enabled me to approach, to get through
the crowd. A folding seat had been reserved for me so that I would
take the microphone in front of a thousand of people. It was moving:
people were shouting and chanting my name. There was so much
noise that it was impossible for me to get a word in edgeways. I had
arrived with Jelle and company. Marc Coucke, our boss, had given
a barrel beer for the first served. It hadn't lasted for long! After, I let
myself be cradled by the euphoria, by the plenitude, by feelings that
are hard to express, to explain, perhaps even to understand. I had
said that it was the most beautiful race of the world. For me, perhaps
not for the others but so what? I had finally won it. Perhaps I'll never
win the Liege-Bastogne-Liege again? So I shared that sacred day with
my supporters, and then later as a family. With my young brother
Jerome, his girlfriend Sophie, my friend Vincent Wathelet and his
partner Winny, and Dirk De Wolf who spent a few minutes with
us, we uncorked a bottle of pink Champagne, my favourite, on the
terrace of my house in Havelange (Harzé). From there, I could still
hear the songs, the whoops and the music coming from La Redoute.
I looked at the sky, with a champagne glass in my hand. The sky
had a summertime clearness, which was impressive. I thought of
my grandparents in the cemetery, of Patricia and Alan from whom
I was separated by the effervescence of the media and the protocol,
of all of my people, of this incredible fortnight since the Brabant
Arrow. Should I thank anybody? Yes, my entire team, its staff, and its
managers. Without them, none of it would have been possible. May
it also be said in passing: I was proud to wear the Omega Pharma-
Lotto colours, the ugliest jersey of the Vélo-Magazine peloton, because
for always, I will salute the trust and the motivation of the entire
managerial staff. To thank my family, my wife, my close relations, my
friends, and destiny for having given me all that, even though I had
worked for it... My emotion was extreme and when I went to sleep, I
knew that I had accomplished a large part of my destiny.'

CHAPTER 14

The Merry Month of May!

Easter Monday is great for those who haven't had much sleep. On La Redoute, one has to tidy up, clear away, forget the... 15,000 litres of beer, an absolute record, which had flowed during the Easter weekend. Philippe hadn't had much sleep, but he was not intending to rest. In the morning, despite the bank holiday, he went with Vincent Wathelet to the National Lottery offices. Although it was not yet official, the future separation between Omega Pharma and Lotto was known in cycling circles. This situation considerably changed the hand for the World Number One's future.

'Vincent, my mentor from Monaco'

'Since that time, Vincent Wathelet's name has often been mentioned in the Press. It's high time that I spoke about him! First, he's not my manager, which will enable everyone to have the definitive information on the subject, but a friend whom I met in Monaco when I was still with La Française des Jeux. I had briefly met him, in 2005, during a prize-giving ceremony in Paris when I had won the final ranking of the French Cup. Marc Madiot had introduced him to me as the 'crazy Belgian' but we left it at that, we had hardly exchanged any words. A good two years later, I saw him again, by the greatest of chance! It was on a Tuesday, I had remained in the south after the Paris-Nice rather than going up into the Belgian cold and I had asked Stéphane Thirion to help me by driving me around and by finding me a hotel. However, he had had a dinner date on that particular Tuesday with Vincent, whom he had known for many a long year. Initially, I was tired and I hadn't wanted to accompany him, and then I changed my mind at the last moment! I discovered a television man, a producer of images, somebody full of life, humour, and knowledge. I above all met someone simple and endearing. I

connected with him because he was from Seraing, he had kept his Liege accent, and I therefore spent an enjoyable evening in the Paris Casino's brasserie. It was a few days before the Milan-San Remo. I was at the time having my first contacts with Lotto: to be precise, I hadn't yet studied anything, I was reflecting. Vincent soon made me appreciate Monaco by extolling the climate and the training conditions to me. It was a pivotal period for me: I had bought a house in Havelange, but I fully realised that it would be much nicer to train on the Riviera in winter rather than in our Ardennes. From there to settling in Monaco was but a single step. When I had finally decided to sign for Lotto, Vincent convinced me to settle on the Coast. He found me a flat, a mechanic, a trainer, and all those details that obsess a cyclist's life, in record time. I was given preferential treatment, Patricia accompanied me: it wasn't easy for her to leave her family because it all happened very quickly. Since then, Vincent has inevitably remained my informed advisor but I will finish this aside by specifying that he does not have the function of manager as it is perceived today in sports circles. To make things even clearer, I don't have a manager. But I listen to some trustworthy people who surround me. I also listen to my brother Christian, my first mentor, who often has a pertinent opinion. Therefore, on that Easter Monday, we listened to the Lottery's arguments. They told us that in 2012 it would be a new start, a new team without Omega. But with whom? At that time, Marc Frederix (the Marketing Director at the National Lottery) was unable to answer and we regretted the fact. It all took place in a polite atmosphere, I think that I've already said it, but I've never had the least enmity with Marc Frederix, quite the reverse, he is somebody whom I like.

'At that time, it should be known that all the World Tour teams except for Euskaltel and Lampre had already approached me. I had answered all the team managers by telephone, e-mail or text: that was just minimal politeness. I was in fact a little disconcerted by the divorce between Omega Pharma and Lotto because, you wouldn't think it, but we had built something solid and sustainable together. I had seen myself finishing my career in style there by setting the

bar even higher, by advocating the adoption of young cyclists. At the human level, I had experienced some great moments in that team, I'll never be able to forget them, we have all evolved together, we have all progressed together, Jürgen, Jelle, Olivier etc. Omega Pharma-Lotto finished the season as Number One, which is quite something for the sponsors, and for the managers who had invested their time, patience and knowledge. It was a little sad to finish like that being cut off in front, a little like at HTC, which disappeared all of a sudden. It was especially sad and regrettable for those who would find themselves on the dole, be they riders or members of the management.'

'The meeting however turned sour when Dirk Messens, the National Lottery's Legal Director, literally put pressure on me to decide. I practically had to give my answer that very day ! I reckoned that I had the right to study the other proposals; my future was at stake, in particular the finest sporting years of my career. The matter even became virulent, and I still haven't understood why. So much so that Marc Frederix apologised, although he hadn't needed to. So I got out of there, the winner of the Liege-Bastogne-Liege the day before but a little dis-enchanted, it was the last straw ! On reflection, I even think that it was the worst day of my 2011 year. They held out a biro to me so that I would sign, almost with a knife to my throat, and, to be frank, I didn't like it. I wasn't ready for such a tough meeting, I was tired, I needed to release the pressure after a crazy period. I still fail to understand how the managers who imposed such pressure on me couldn't see that, at the human level.'

A Quick Trip to Copenhagen

Disillusioned on leaving the Lottery's offices, Philippe rested because, the following day, he had to fly to Copenhagen, heading for Rudersdal and a reccy of the world championships circuit accompanied by Tom Boonen and Jelle Wallays.

'The date had been scheduled for a long time, so there was no question of withdrawing even though I was tired. That allows me another

aside because I'm asked a thousand times: do I get on well with Tom Boonen? Yes, we're not friends in everyday life but we respect each other and, when we see each other, we don't inevitably talk about cycling. He for example said nothing to me about my victory in Liege, although it was only two days later, as I had said nothing to him after his victories in the past. We are professionals: victory, defeat and training are all part of our trade. We're all winners of something, so there's no point in making a meal of it. Incidentally, we discovered our future hotel for the world championships and the local food was very interesting. I had made enquiries and I knew that the best restaurant in the world is in Copenhagen but I doubt that we would be invited to it! Moreover, I love the new cuisine, the herbs, the natural essences: they give the dishes a fabulous taste.'

'I haven't been a fan of the course since the first tour, it's true, but I reckoned that the ascending arrival could open every scenario. Actually, I wasn't yet "in it" four months in advance. The local television and radio stations were there, we gave some interviews and I told myself that I was so tired that it was impossible for me to have an objective opinion about the course. And then October was a long way away...'

'I was in a hurry for one thing only: to return to Monaco to have a rest, and to see Patricia and Alan again. Meanwhile, the telephone was getting hot for my transfer: Vincent was taking care of it. I didn't want to precipitate anything. The priority in my mind was to study each proposal and to answer everyone. I had received some long messages, like those from Vincent Lavenu (AG2R) or Eric Boyer (Cofidis), and I had the great surprise of having the boss of Team Sky in person on the telephone. There was BMC, also, but it was not the most aggressive team, at the beginning, for having me. There was finally Patrick Lefevere to whom I would like to say, via this book, that I have never broken my word or committed an act of treason. On the contrary, I respected his offer and his ideas on cycling, but OK, it didn't happen.'

'In Monaco, I took a breather, I benefited from it. It's the only region
of Old Europe where you can drink a coffee on a terrace without being
disturbed. During training, when I go into Italy, I'm applauded
by the Italians who recognise me. They shout "Liegi"! (Liege), I
know that for them, winning the Doyenne is an institution like the
Lombardy. It is sacred and I really like those traditions anchored
in the history of cycling, and it's always nice to be recognized in
a country where they love high-level sportsmen whatever their
nationality. I had a one-week break, however, after Copenhagen:
no cycling. I benefited from the normal life of a young husband and
father, which had been exceptional for me since the beginning of the
year. At the dietary level, I was exercising a rare vigilance: I was
eating very little, avoiding starchy foods and especially alcohol. Like
everyone, I like a good glass of wine but in the non-racing period. I
had even... lost weight, even though I wasn't riding! One should not
get too thin either and lose ones muscle, I take care of all those details,
I purge my body of its toxins then I resume the training with my usual
friends. As I do at the beginning of season with gentle periods of two
to three hours towards Antibes and Juan-les-Pins.'

'The Shock of Weylandt's Death'

'One day, I was going to ride with Stuart O'Grady, which we hadn't
done for many a long week. He's a nice guy with whom I have
excellent contacts but our programmes had been different. I don't
know why, on that day precisely (09 May), but we started to talk
about Wouter Weylandt while riding. Stuart had welcomed him at
Leopard and he explained to me that the change of team had done
him some good, that he had m enormous progress and that in his
Luxembourg formation, he could take his chance as a sprinter. I came
home from the training a few hours later and turned the television on
to Eurosport. Jacky Durand was talking all the time about Weylandt,
he said that his fall was serious but that he didn't know any more
about it. The TV images didn't bring any more information. Then
his death was announced. I was in shock, really pale, at home. I called

Stuart O'Grady: he was destroyed. I very often think of that day of 09 May because I still have no explanation as to why Stuart and I, who were no longer accustomed to training together very often, had decided to talk about Wouter. Was it pure chance? I'm not certain. However, I wasn't a close friend of Weylandt, I would come across him in the peloton, I would chew the fat with him but I hadn't had his phone number. He was a pleasant chap - open, nice, ambitious, and talented. I of course sent to a short note to his family, to his supporters, his friends, and his colleagues. For the riders who live in the middle of the peloton, a fatal fall in a race is something that haunts you. It's rare, fortunately, I had known that of Kivilev in the Paris-Nice, and now that of Wouter. I was in the race, once again in the Giro, in 2009, when Pedro Horrillo had a horrible fall into a ravine. It was very serious: he came out of it alive but he had to give up cycling.'

'So, do we take risks each day in a race? The proportion of fatal accidents in a cycle race compared to the number of deaths on the road in cars is obviously largely in "favour" of the latter. So the situation should not be dramatised. The more so as the real risks are not taken on the descents. Because there, you control them, you adapt a safety distance even if risks are taken, I admit it, as in the Cipressa for example, at the end of the Milan-San Remo. The real danger, for me, is the massive sprint at 70 kph where we're all shoulder to shoulder. There, nothing is controlled, you try to control your path and your machine, but it's not easy.'

The death of Wouter Weylandt, at the end of an exceptional Belgian season, reminds us, above all, that it was also dramatic with the tragic disappearance of that gentleman from Ghent, the great friend of Tyler Farrar. Nobody will forget him and this book can only pay him homage.

CHAPTER 15

My Revenge in the Tour of Belgium

When the start of the Tour of Belgium arrived on 25 May, that is to say one month after the triumph of the Liege-Bastogne-Liege, everyone was thinking of Wouter Weylandt, winner of the opening Ostend stage three years previously. At the Buggenhout start where the prologue was contested under ideal conditions, one could clearly perceive the trauma left by the tragic departure of the man from Ghent among the registered riders, including Tom Boonen and Stijn Devolder, who were visibly affected by the disappearance of their friend.

Phil, for his part, returned as the absolute star. His exceptional spring had endeared him to the hearts of all cycling lovers. World Number One, unbeaten since his victory in the Brabant Arrow, his stature had immensely increased. The separation between Omega Pharma and Lotto, now completely official, had opened the door to every fabrication, in the Press, which was quoting the man from Remouchamps practically everywhere. The tension was mounting on a subject where everyone was looking for a scoop: where would Philippe be riding in 2012?

'In Monaco, I hadn't been aware of the extent of the pressure even though I had kept abreast, albeit distractedly, of what was being said and written. During my last week of training before coming back up to my country, I had intensified the programme. I had even imposed some very hard exercises on myself in the mountains around my home. I had also multiplied my training sessions on the stopwatch bike. I knew that the Tour of Belgium included an opening prologue and it is perhaps the most complicated stage for me, the one where I could lose the general classification. Because I was clearly coming to win. It was now a month since I had last raced, but I had looked after myself properly, and I had trained well.'

No Dauphiné and no Tour of Switzerland

On the eve of the prologue, in Ghent, Philippe received the Press to speak about his immediate ambitions. '*Omega Pharma-Lotto has a duty to shine in the Tour of Belgium with Greipel, Roelandts and myself insofar as our team has proved that it was the best in Belgium. It is all the more mandatory as our Lotto sponsor is one of the event's partners. We have the possibility of playing in several scenes. I can, as far as I'm concerned, aim for a stage victory at Eupen: it's an arrival that I know, and one that suits me. And perhaps the final classification if things go well! Many were worried about the lightness of my programme before the Tour De France (Tour of Belgium, Ster Elektro Tour) but what could I have done in the mountains of the Dauphiné Rally or the Tour of Switzerland except exhaust myself on the passes? I have more and more the impression that all the organizers want to propose the hardest race, as if it had to be aligned on the Giro. Unlike our leader, Jurgen Van den Broeck, who will have to be at 98% at the beginning of the first stage in order to be on top in the high mountains, I for my part will have to be at 100% immediately since my objectives will be in place from the start. This is the reason why I've chosen a preparation that's, let's say, out of sync. It will be seen later whether or not I've been right but I don't need to go up the Alpe d'Huez at 45kph!*'

On excellent form behind the microphone that day, Phil sent out a message that would be front-page news, the following day, in the Press. '*What do I have to complain about? However, I believe that our sport is in danger, the sponsors are disappearing. It needed the unfortunate death of Wouter Weylandt to measure the solidarity of the peloton but, for the rest, there's nevertheless a lot of "every man for himself". We're in a pivotal period for cycling: races are taking shape and being organised on every continent, that's fine in the context of globalization, but I have the feeling that people are forgetting that the riders are men and that they cannot perform well in Australia, China, the United States and Europe all in the same season.*'

In Buggenhout, the streets are too narrow to accommodate the large crowd scattered between the start and the arrival of the 5,600 metres of the opening stopwatch event.

0.71 of a second behind Westra

'In relation to this race, I'm also a little angry because, the previous year, I had lost it for two reasons: the rain that had made its appearance during the against-the-clock of Herzele when I was the leader, and that famous puncture during the queen stage when I had to wait an insane amount of time before being repaired when I was in front, on the attack. I don't like to dwell on failures for which I'm not responsible. During my warm-up, I had respected a formula that Gert Steegmans had dictated to me about during a training session in Monaco. I was pretty content with his advice but I was to take care not to reveal its secret! In any case, my efforts were not in vain; I had felt really good during that short stopwatch event that had suited me rather well because it was very technical, with many bends. There was a headwind in certain places and, moreover, I didn't take too many risks as I had the rest of the event in my mind.'

By getting himself classified at 0.71 of a second, or a cat's whisker, behind the Dutch winner Lieuwe Westra (Vacansoleil), Philippe had marked people's minds. Because many were already thinking of the Walloon stage of Eupen where, on paper, he had no rival.

The following day, at the Lochristi start, a radical change of scene. The wind was blowing violently and the sprinters, who had already been rubbing their hands when viewing the course towards Knokke, were looking down in the dumps. There was a strong smell of 'edges': there was tension in the peloton. The side wind was blowing, indeed, and Phil in person had done the housework to dislocate the group. Westra, like his leader Devolder, spent a quarter of an hour when the first peloton arrived at the foot of the 'Poggio of Knokke' in Duinbergen. The anticipated duel between Greipel and Boonen turned clearly to the German's advantage, very powerful in his finishing.

'For us, it is obviously a bonus. Andre too had had to get ready for the fray before the Tour De France, to reassure his team mates on his state of form and he did so very well by taking the leader's jersey into the bargain. The stage between Knokke and Ypres comprised the Mont-Kemmel ascent, on the Friday. I took the bonus points but I hadn't inevitably wanted to take the leader's jersey, I thought that

Greipel would keep it at the end of the sprint but it was Kruopis (the Lithuanian from the Landbouwkrediet team) who had imposed himself. As a result, I took possession of the black jersey for a second place over my German teammate. That irritated me more than anything else on the day before the stage between Bertem and Eupen that I wanted to win because that obliged us to face up to our responsibilities more, but we were there for that.'

My meeting with Frank Vandenbroucke's mother

'In Ypres, after having received the bouquet from the hands of the Prime Minister, Yves Leterme, I had an impromptu appointment and hurriedly got ready in a little room in the Town Hall. Stéphane Thirion had warned me, the previous day, of the presence of Chantal Vandenbroucke, Frank's mother, at the arrival. She wanted to meet me, and vice versa. Initially, we had made an appointment in the team bus because I hadn't thought that I would be taking part in the protocol that day but, finally, it was better thus. Moreover, my parents were there too: they had chosen to follow the entire Tour of Belgium and to spend each night in an hotel, an adventure for them ! In the intimacy of that little room, without the presence of the Press, I experienced a very moving moment. In fact, Chantal had one day obtained my phone number and, each time I won a race, she regularly sent me messages of encouragement and/or congratulations. I found it touching and I answered each time. I don't know whether my actions brought a kind of ray of sunshine into her heart, but I took it as that. I had been overwhelmed like everyone else by Frank's death. I had met him for a fairly long time during Nico Mattan's farewells after the Franco-Belgian event. He fascinated me even though he was only a shadow of his former self. His popularity, especially in Flanders, impressed me. As soon as he set foot in a Flemish village, there was effervescence. "Franky Boy", as they called him, was their idol. A few days before his death, I had had a chat with him in Lugano where he had accompanied the Belgian delegation to the world championships of Mendrisio. I had found him on form, rather honed, with a desire

to resume the competition in a new team. Often, I'm compared to him. People believe that I had replaced him in the Walloon peloton. I don't like that notion. I don't resemble him at all, nobody will ever resemble him, each has his own style and his own personality. For me, Frank will always remain the one who had won the Liege-Bastogne-Liege in 1999. I was a kid: I had watched that with eyes filled with wonder with the well-anchored dream of doing likewise one day. When I had given my bouquet to Chantal, encouraged by my mother who was expecting only that, I felt a great deal of emotion invading the room in Ypres. I liked that moment a lot: I will remember it for a long time. I also know that that bouquet went straight on to Frank's tomb. My relationship with his parents is truly sincere. Moreover, these people know cycling and love it: everyone knows what the Vandenbroucke family represents in Belgian cycling.'

Philippe had the black jersey on the morning of the Bertem to Eupen stage: no more obviously was needed to assemble a huge crowd on the course.

'I had already felt it before but there, it was very clear: everyone was riding against me, against us (Omega Pharma-Lotto) generally. It was rather complicated. On the Haute Levée, I had reckoned that my team mates had already given a great deal, so I took the initiative of the race rather early so that the others could keep their strength for the following day. Despite several Rabobank men hard on my tail, I had practically climbed the entire Mont Righi, in the Fagnes, in the front without being relieved. It's a hill that I know very well, it suits me perfectly as a course for my training because it is excessively long. When I was an amateur, I would climb it flat out, so I had an advantage over the others, whose tongues were hanging out. I was in top gear, in the last two kilometres, my speedometer indicated between 40 and 45 kph. It did me good to annoy my competitors. They had wanted my hide by isolating me very early, but I gave them my answer, because attack is the best defence. People talk of "revenge" or pride, that's OK by me. Pride is essential in sport. If you are too nice, you get walked over. But after a race, I am myself, I haven't changed even though I'm Number One, and I remain close to people.

In Eupen, it was a long sprint, my supporters were there, it was really great, it reminded me of April. I had beaten Van Avermaet, Leukemans and De Waele, the organizers were content since they had only "Belgians" in front ! On that particular day, I knew that I would win: I was even almost too sure of myself. I expected only one thing, the finishing line, and the race seemed to me to be interminable. I know that being too sure of myself will play tricks on me but when you feel that feeling, you have to take advantage of it. And that's what I've done this season.'

In Putte, the team's triumph was complete: Greipel had added a second stage victory to his week, the sun was shining, Phil was radiant and, in the little school classroom that served as a press room, for the first time since the start of the 'rumours', a journalist asked: 'Could you enlighten us about your future, tell us in which team you will be riding?' *'I have nothing to say about that, I want to be serene, to prepare for the Tour De France in peace and quiet. We'll see later.'*

Without knowing it, Phil had just started the beginning of a serial which was to be the talk of the town, because everyone wanted to know in which team he would be riding in 2012...

CHAPTER 16

The Ster Electro Tour As Well!

For Philippe to be victorious in a stage race was not routine, usually because they include a fairly long against-the-clock event in the middle. But he had worked on that particularity. *'And I'm counting on working even more on it in 2012 on my stopwatch bike, because I know and feel that this is the moment to invest my forces in this exercise that can prevent a rider from being complete if he's not suitably fast against the clock.'* In the aftermath of the Tour of Belgium, which had assembled a considerable crowd, Phil remained faithful to his customary practices. One of them consists of taking part in the race of Gullegem, where the festival of cycling, down there, is not an empty word. The event also accommodates amateurs, which allows Jerome, his younger brother (19 months younger), to ride with his champion sibling. *'When Philippe and Jerome were small, they deployed so much energy that I sometimes had to keep them on a leash',* their father Jeannot often recalls with a smile.

> *'On that particular day, we had gone out as a family. My other brother, Christian, had bet on me in a local bookmaker's, you know, those people who deposit an enormous slate in front of a table with the riders' odds written in chalk. I had won but the fellow, a crook, had fled at the end of the race! A race where Jerome had broken his wheel against Boonen's, which he's never forgotten. People often ask me what I'm doing in a race of this kind. I do it not only to please the organizer or the public, but also to accomplish 200 kilometres at an intensive pace, because in those events, there's no calculation, there's no tactic against any particular individual. The guys race flat out and the "big guns" logically emerge at the end. Moreover, I don't take any risks. I train, in a way, by taking care not to fall sick.'*

Leaving Gullegem, Phil also made a detour via Calais, another rally, which he also won. There, also, it's a respect for custom.

'I get an exceptional welcome there every time. I owe it to Philippe Crepel, the former rider, sports manager and ex-manager of Laurent Jalabert. A man who counts, in the North of France, in cycling circles, and who is also the best friend of Jean-Marie Leblanc, which is no small reference.'

It was time to return to Monaco. The countdown to the Tour De France was underway. While the others were working on the roads of the Dauphiné or the Tour of Switzerland, he had chosen the Ster Electro Tour, that modest Belgo-Dutch event that he had already won ahead of Niki Terpstra in 2009. *'There were certainly a couple of stages that could have suited me in the Dauphiné or in Switzerland, but generally, it was too hard. So I knowingly chose a lighter programme. Five days, that was my cup of tea, it suited me perfectly because I also had in mind, well before thinking of the Tour, the championships of Belgium in Hooglede. However, I knew that the tricolour jersey would be played for on courses that resemble the narrow roads of the Ster Electro Tour. Neglect no detail, as I often tell myself. It is quickly forgotten that I had completed the entire campaign of the classics, unlike certain riders who just come to win the Tour De France. So I above all had to save myself, to be fresh, physically and mentally. And then I also wanted to have some fun, to win. The Ster Electro Tour, if the team is up for it, is something special for me. Before, I used to insist on large workloads before the Tour, and that didn't work for me. And if I will be short of references in relation to the high mountains, I point out that nobody has asked me to climb the Galibier more quickly than Contador. Me, I want to be fresh and to have strength in my legs at very precise moments during the first two weeks. I had won a stage in the Giro and some others in the Vuelta, but never in the Tour, so it was a major objective. Not being in the Dauphiné or in Switzerland also removed the pressure, especially from the Press. And to go and do the gruppetto every day? No, thank you very much.'*

But on the subject of pressure, it was just the opposite that occurred. Because, for a few days, a veritable mania had gripped the media. Each wanted to be the first to know where Phil would be going in 2012. Astana, BMC and Sky were mentioned in bulk. A Lotto-Belgacom association was also mentioned, due to the fact that the Belgian telecom operator has just lost the retransmission rights for football matches in Belgium. Would it invest in cycling? Each gave his or her opinion: the tension mounted.

'I try as best I can to avoid reading all that but it's difficult. I realise above all that beyond knowing where I will be riding in 2012, whole pages are written on my private life, on my lifestyle in Monaco, on some incredible things. I've always wanted a simple and discreet life but I find myself almost every day on the front pages of the Press. The journalists suppose things and, if they're mistaken, they don't not bother to set the record straight the following day. They even mention the amount of my future salary, and the make of my car. There, I cracked, I was distraught and disgusted. Previously, I appreciated the interviewing process. It was something pleasant, constructive and enriching, but there, everything is being done to make me distance myself from the Press, whereas I had always wanted to maintain cordial relations with it.'

My Anger Against The Press

When Phil says that he cracked, it was not an empty word.

'I couldn't stand it any longer. A press conference had been organised in the NH Hotel in Maastricht (yes, there once again), in the middle of the Ster Electro Tour. Basically it was to evoke the championships of Belgium because I would not thereafter have any more time to devote to the Press as of the moment when I would return to Monaco to come back again on the Saturday, the eve of the Belgium championships. But I had asked Marc Sergeant to take the floor to evoke something else before the journalists. I hadn't prepared anything, I didn't have a piece of paper in front of me and I launched out!' In fact, nobody had ever seen Philippe in this situation before. What he had to say was clear, concise, precise, and direct!

'I would like to ask you to stop publishing fantasies about my future every day. I read what is written, some true things, but I mainly read some totally unreal things. That's not good for me, nor for my team, nor for my team mates. I am at the end of my contract, it's true. It is also true that I have received proposals from everyone except Lampre

and Euskaltel. Out of respect, I have met the managers of each team,
and then I have set aside the proposals that did not correspond with
my philosophy. My priority is to listen, in the first place, to my current
employers, Omega Pharma and Lotto, who are going to separate.
I would have liked to have been settled before the championship of
Belgium, but events will defer this timeframe beyond the Tour. My
best years are ahead of me, and I don't want to make a wrong choice.
I need to choose the team that will offer me team mates of the right
quality because a good teammate is worth more than money. Four or
five teams are still in contention according to what Omega Pharma
and Lotto will do on their side. I also want to build something, to
bring my experience, motivation, mentality and advice to the group
that will be welcoming me. The problem for us is that Omega Pharma
and Lotto are not leaving cycling: they are separating. We therefore
have to continue to work in a tricky environment. Finally, I would
love to receive 3.5 million a year, as I read from some of you. Give
those completely foolish figures a rest ! This auction is unacceptable.
Me, I want a long-term contract in a serious team, with optimal
management and team mates of the right quality. In relation to
the interest expressed by Patrick Lefevere, that constitutes one of the
proposals that I have received.' For the first time, Philippe spoke of
some interest from Quick Step. The secret had been more or less
well kept up to that point. But nobody knew, at that moment,
that the former divorcees (Coucke, Omega Pharma) and Lefevere
(Quick Step) were about to kiss and make up. Despite Philippe's
emphatic request, the very next day, a newspaper announced that
the man from Remouchamps would be riding for the American
BMC team as from 2012. His message calling for peace and quiet
had not therefore been received loud and clear.

'Since then, certain journalists think that I hate them. I don't hate anybody
but I don't like people who disappoint me and, there, I was disappointed. And
when I am, it's for a long time. Because, when I give, I do so without concession,
to the full, from my heart. Here, I have the impression of having been betrayed:
I had believed that journalists had more probity. However, they were more
interested in the purchase of my Audi rather than in my place of World Number

One, all at about ten days from the start of the Tour. Sickening!' Two days
earlier, in Alblasserdam, in the affluent suburbs of Rotterdam where there
are boats moored that would delight the most selective yachtsmen, Philippe
was warming up on a makeshift car park for the prologue of the Ster Electro
Tour contested during the previous evening, a formula allowed by the long
days of June. The wind was severe, the course too rectilinear. The observers
were struck by a particular detail: the stopwatch bike, black, coloured by a
blue logo in italics – 'Philfast'. *'I like to take care of my look and therefore of
that of my equipment. Canyon was in agreement about my bicycle's new look,
and I could choose all the details. The blue was to recall the national team's
jersey: I like that colour. I had also asked for the "silver grey" check, which
is in fact a copy of the design of my favourite car, the Porsche GT3 RS! This
stopwatch bike was not made for me: I ceilinged fairly quickly on the flat. That
was no doubt normal after having given so much in explosiveness exercises on
the hills. But I was not displeased with my result. In relation to other favourites
of the final ranking, 17th, at 18 seconds behind Patrick Gretsch, a young
German specialist in the HTC team, wasn't too bad. Even though I was a few
seconds behind the two potential favourites, the Dutch Langeveld and Terpstra.'*

Philippe was right to be wary of them because in the first stage towards
Sittard, Phil played the "King of the Mountains" (the polka dot jersey) and
realised that the Dutchmen were motivated. At the arrival, a great moment
of emotion swept through the spectators when Tyler Farrar clearly outdid
Romain Feillu in the sprint. That wasn't much of a feat except that, for the
first time since Wouter Weylandt's fatal accident, the American raised his
arms on the finishing line and found a little smile once again. Furthermore,
he was to mention Wouter incessantly after the arrival in a simple but terribly poignant confession, which left the observers deeply moved by the
Garmin-Cervélo sprinter's abundant humanity. Phil, for his part, donned
the polka dot jersey. If someone had told him on that day that he would be
donning the same one in the Tour De France a few weeks later...

The following day, during the stage that connected Schimmert to Schimmert,
in a pale imitation of the Amstel Gold Race, since the riders crossed the
Cauberg at Valkenburg, the hoped fight didn't materialize. *'Everyone was
expecting that our team would race although we didn't have the leader's jersey,*

which took the biscuit all the same! But it was proof that the adversaries believed that I was the favourite and that I had, at any time, to assume my responsibilities. That didn't bother me but I never understand the tactics of certain teams that sacrifice their own interests when they could win a stage or something else.'

It was therefore Omega Pharma-Lotto rather than HTC or Rabobank, or even Garmin, that was to attempt a second success of Farrar which started when the breakaway's lead became too great. *'David Boucher stuck to it. On his own, he made up three minutes on the attackers, which meant that they weren't riding that quickly in front either. Then, I still let things happen and then they finally started to move.'* In the Cauberg, very precisely, where Phil had been unbeaten since April 2010, Leukemans sparked off an explosion. The Belgian de Vacansoleil that Gilbert had for several years dreamt of having as a teammate made his compatriot come out of his box and there was no delay because fifteen riders detached themselves. Gilbert, Leukemans, but also Terpstra and Tankink. Fifteen of them, they flew towards Schimmert where Phil won the bonus points at the time of the first crossing of the finishing line. Three seconds, in such a tight race, is never a trifle.

> *'However, at the beginning, I hadn't ridden in the breakaway group because, on Thursday, the others hadn't done so. They had been a little disconcerted: it's not always for me to do the work. After, each had done his own, but with the HTC, Sky and Garmin that were riding behind, it had become a little complicated. I had tried to avoid the massive sprint at 600 metres from the goal but I was caught and there, I got going.'* In order to assist, from behind, in the success of the Argentinian Juan-Jose Haedo, a sprinter who never hesitates to take his chance when the heavyweights of his discipline are not there. And as Tyler Farrar was not involved, the Saxo Bank rider threw himself into the opening. *'Terpstra and Tankink seemed to be clinging on, so they would have to be attacked towards La Gileppe. Moreover, rain and wind were announced, it would be a lovely brawl, with the same context: we would have to assume our responsibilities. In 2004, in the same stage, the breakaway group had left after five kilometres! I therefore had no plan, except to ride in front: it's always the best tactic.'*

Verviers, My Birthplace

'On that particular day, I had some extraordinary feelings, a kind of certainty that it is difficult to explain in sport. The fourth stage started from Verviers and that meant a lot for me, since I was born there, on 05 July 1982! At the start, there were about thirty young riders from the Ardennes CC who were waiting for me for autographs and photographs. It was raining a lot, I liked that atmosphere and, moreover, the race went over La Redoute. It had nothing to do with the Liege-Bastogne-Liege, of course, but I was all the same at home, and many supporters were there. I knew the arrival well: it was the same as in 2009. The guys were flat out as from the Maquisard. We then crossed a hill in Spa that I know well, but which was no longer part of the professional races, Annette and Lubin. I didn't suffer from the absence of the earpiece since I knew it all by heart! Before climbing Annette and Lubin, the team had split the peloton in Avenue Reine Astrid in Spa. Collectively, it was still a great performance. I remember in particular the work of Bart De Clercq and Klaas Lodewyck. If one had to give a cycling lesson in a school, I would certainly choose this fourth stage of the Ster Electro Tour for talking to the youngsters and for showing them what had to be done. On La Gileppe, under a flood of rain, I stuck to Niki Terpstra like in 2009, except that this time, thanks to the bonus points, I'm in front and I take the jersey. It still had to be kept and therefore defended.'

In the Etten-Leur stage, on the following day in the Netherlands, the rain had not taken any rest. It whipped the soaked faces of the riders, obliged to take a practically flooded paved path in order to go to sign the starting sheet.

'I was still at the mercy of a bonus point in relation to Terpstra. At the beginning, there was a breakaway group, which suited us well, then at the time of the second sprint, I won ahead of Lodewyck who had taken me along perfectly. Terpstra reproached us for having boxed him in but that reflection was due to his frustration because we had manoeuvred properly. I came out of it exhausted, in every sense of the word, but still unbeaten since the Brabant Arrow. I was in a hurry for only one thing, to get back to the sun of Monaco, even if I hadn't wasted my time. One never knows, if the weather is bad in the Brittany stages of the Tour De France, I will have had a little training for taking the water!'

CHAPTER 17

The World's Most Beautiful Jersey

The ghastly weather of the Ster Electro Tour gave not the slightest glimpse of the beginning of a resplendent summer. However, all of a sudden, the sun arrived with its rays and some lovely prospects. In the little commune of Hooglede-Gits, where cyclo-cross is usually king, the last Sunday of June is devoted to the championship of Belgium, as furthermore tradition in all the countries of 'Old Europe' so requires. After two editions on the fairly serious reliefs, Aywaille and Leuven, the organizers were proposing a virtual ironing board by way of a belgo-Belgian contest. Despite everything, Philippe Gilbert's supremacy was such that this course for sprinters did not remove him from the list of pretenders. On the contrary, it was significant to note on the morning of the appointment that all the specialists had chosen him as favourite with astonishing unanimity. Why? Partly because Belgium was looking for a pure sprinter, and then because the Boonen-Steegmans pair at Quick Step didn't seem to be above the fray, quite the opposite. *For the moment, Phil can win everything'*, Boonen furthermore explained in an interview, a question also of heaping the pressure on his rival. Bjorn Leukemans' opinion was more nuanced: *'When he says that he's not the favourite, Phil is playing mind-games with his adversaries. I don't believe him for a second!'*

'If I can give pleasure to a teammate...'

'After a short week in Monaco which I knew would be the last since it was the Tour De France thereafter, I had arrived very relaxed at the start. On the Saturday, we did some super training with the team, which I felt was very motivated. The weather conditions were ideal and, as far as my fitness was concerned, it was precisely what I had wanted for that appointment. The circuit was flat but it was long and I had nevertheless won in Gullegem. I confirm that one never wastes ones time by taking part from time to time in what

people still sometimes call a "village fair". The rhythm that we will give to the race, the heat and the attacks on a circuit that is not all that technically accommodating will determine everything At the Omega Pharma-Lotto team briefing, we of course knew that we had an advantage in numbers compared to certain isolated runners but that meant nothing, as would be seen later furthermore with Meersman on the podium. Marc Sergeant had asked the team to ride for me but I had corrected that requirement. Because my team mates had already served me proud since the beginning of the season. I was rather in an opposite scheme: if I could give pleasure to a fast man such as Roelandts or Dehaes, who was going well at that time, I wouldn't hesitate. A place on a championship podium is also a guarantee for the future and therefore of a contract to be renewed or acquired. Some should benefit from it. But, to take a sprinter along, one must inevitably be there at the end! I had never been the champion of Belgium but four times on the podium, and that was missing from my record. And I wanted it a lot because the Belgian jersey is the peloton's most beautiful one. The black, yellow and red make a good match on a tunic that is worn for a year. It's also the jersey of the country of the bicycle, Belgium. But it's perhaps the most complicated race to gain. Eddy Merckx conquered it only once. And Boonen had beaten me in Aywaille on possibly the most selective circuit of recent years! But I couldn't see myself finishing my career without having worn that jersey at least once! I think that my words had pleased the other riders: they were surprised, to some extent, that I had offered them almost a free hand, but I meant it.'

Around Roulers, where the motorway exits are as numerous as the branches of a poplar, it was a free-for-all, monstrous traffic jams created by a lack of clear signposting. Moreover, the organizers had chosen to ask for an entrance fee, which is fairly rare in cycling, which accentuated still further the slowdowns on the approach of Hooglede-Gits, where a huge crowd was waiting for the riders. The weather was splendid, even straightforwardly tropical, judging the noses that were quickly coloured by the sun and... by the lager. Among the supporters who hoisted their flags as high as possible to proclaim their choice, it could be seen that the majority was expecting a

Boonen-Gilbert match. Like two years earlier, in Aywaille, where in front
of the astounded guard of his sympathisers who had been on duty since
the early morning, the man from Antwerp came to deprive Phil of a pre-
announced party. That episode has, ever since, been playing on the mind of
the man from the Ardennes. The following year, he had left from a long way
away, in Leuven, and had perhaps wasted his cartridges to allow Devolder to
finish as he had done. *'It was perhaps for that, even certainly, that the circuit
in Hooglede suited me: I finally had less pressure but undoubtedly the best team
that day. Then, as the first laps went by, I finally realised that the circuit was
not as simple as that. The heat and the pace made it more testing than had been
envisaged. Then, we pressed even more on the pedals, setting an infernal rate.
On the technical parts, I saw the guys with their tongues hanging out. I liked all
that until the moment when the traditional breakaway group left and nobody
wanted to relaunch. I had legs of fire and I couldn't bear that situation. I discussed a lot, not only with my team mates but also with riders from other formations, like Staf Scheirlinckx, a guy who can go into the fire if he is motivated.
When Wellens was caught, I lit up with Bakelants, Vanendert and Van de
Walle, who unfortunately fell further on and had to give up. There was also De
Greef, and then Dehaes, who, as I had previously thought, was not bad at all.
We were finally a large group of 18 with all the favourites or almost at 90 kilometres from the arrival: it was incredible all the same on such a circuit. It was
a race of a rare intensity, we had practically never let the others recover. Boonen
and Devolder, my main competitors, were there and were part of the large
breakaway group. Tom had been trapped when it had been formed but, when
he came into it, my speedometer was indicating 58 kph. That is to say that he
was well and that he was going fast. I knew what I was heading for even though
one or other such as Van Hecke had tried. I had in any case only one solution:
to attack on the only 200-metre bump three kilometres from the arrival. It was
that or be beaten. There, my guys were exceptional.'*

Because if Kenny Dehaes, who was to finish 13th, had perhaps had the secret
ambition of sprinting for the victory, it marvellously summarised the state
of freshness and physical form, on that 26 June 2011, of his Omega Pharma-
Lotto leader. *'I was already glad to be in the leading group, to devote myself to
preserving the breakaway group's interest. At the start of the last lap, Philippe
came level with me, almost as if it had just got the start, telling me: "Now we'll*

race"! However, I hadn't really been doing anything else up to that point! Without... Philippe in the breakaway group, I would have had no chance of winning. He was too strong but I wasn't the only one to have felt it.'

Boonen: 'If he leaves me there, I'll give up cycling'

It was furthermore Dehaes who had set the pace in the 'cutlet' which served as the difficulty in the final stretch with Boonen on his wheel and Phil on that of the man form Antwerp, whom he had put to the test where he had decided to. One metre, two then ten, a hundred: the small gap became a gulf. Exhausted by his pursuit race, Boonen did not even do the sprint while his rival, sovereign, treated himself to a sprint of more than two kilometres, managing the bends to perfection.

'Tactically, technically, it was perhaps my masterpiece of the season. It's difficult to compare the victories between themselves but that one was impossible with the only weapon which I had on the final bump but I did it. Everyone was waiting for my attack, Boonen the first, which did not prevent me from succeeding. Later, in Monaco, Steegmans told me a tasty anecdote. At the time of the briefing, at Quick Step, there had been only one watchword: to stick the seat of my pants on the final hill during the last lap. And it's there that Tom Boonen had said to his team mates: "If Gilbert leaves me there, I'll give up cycling". I have not been able to check whether he was going to put his words into action but I hope for him that he wasn't. I've always liked finding myself in a breakaway group with Tom because he participates in it, and usually, it goes right to the end.'

Like in the Paris-Tours, in October 2009, when Phil had taken his first revenge on Tom after the disillusion of Aywaille.

'I was fed up with runner-up places on the podiums of the Belgium championships. It was finally my turn, finally my day in "the" season of my career: that finally flowed from a relentless logic. That tricolour jersey had become a bit of an obsession, I really wanted it very much.

Not only is it beautiful, that jersey, as I've already said, but wearing it remains an honour.'

At six days from the start of the Tour De France, the podium of the Belgium Championship of Hooglede-Gits where the Belgium national anthem was resounding in front of frenzied supporters had a beautiful look with the young Meersman (who learned of his selection for the Tour on behalf of FDJeux a few minutes later), and the promising Jelle Wallays. Phil, for his part, was holding his head with his right hand in his hair. He reckoned that he was dreaming on his feet and that it was not finished. That in a few days, it could remove two colours from beautiful jersey, the red and the black, to keep only one of them: the yellow. But that was still only a dream... that was not crazy at all. In an overheated room during the press conference, just one question was still haunting the journalists beyond the national title that he had just won. 'Have you chosen your team?'

'No ! Some formations are still in contention but I'm giving myself time. It's a question of the contract of my life, of the years that will decide my career with, who knows, a world championship, the Olympic Games, and the classics that I haven't yet been able to land. Although the financial aspect comes into the reckoning, what is paramount for me is the support, which I want to be extremely professional: the equipment, the management, and the team mates. Moreover, I would like to sign a three-year contract, to be protected. Not that I'm planning to rest on my laurels: I can win successes on entry, but that gives me a certain security. And I don't want to talk about it anymore before August the first at the earliest since the ICU regulations stipulate that the transfer market will be officially open on that day.'

By issuing that reflection, Phil wanted to protect himself from any new attempt at a discussion on this debate that was raging in the Press. And he was in a hurry for only one thing in Hooglede: to leave the place to go to savour his success, and his beautiful jersey that he would be able to keep for 365 days. And that he would have the honour of wearing in competition for the first time in the most famous event of the world: the Tour De France !

CHAPTER 18

Finally, the Yellow Jersey!

Emerging from his protocol obligations in Hooglede, Phil was therefore still unbeaten since his victory in the Brabant Arrow. Such longevity is unprecedented in the modern history of cycling. *'After my protocol obligations, the anti-doping procedures and the Press, I was received in the VIP marquis that my team had erected where I spent a further moment, live, for the VRT. I was delighted, happy. Then, I went to my hairdresser, Winny: I've already spoken about her, the partner of my friend Vincent. Because we had made a bet that if I became champion of Belgium, she would dye my hair. We had initially thought of grey, me rather of yellow because the first stage of the Tour was inspiring me enormously. Finally, it was gold-grey yellow, difficult to estimate the colour but so what! I then stayed in Lille before taking the plane for Monaco again. Patricia didn't like my new hairdo at all! I had unfortunately had little time to spend at home, since, as of the following day, I had to be in La Roche-sur-Yon where I was staying with my team. That short family stay however did me a world of good. I was impatient to receive my tricolour jerseys because the only one that I had was dirty and I wanted to train in it: that seemed normal to me! I hadn't been involved in the Tour since 2008. Immediately, when I arrived at the hotel, I found dimension that represented again with all those people around the trucks, who stayed for hours to get a photograph or an autograph.'*

'On the Wednesday, we reccied the team stopwatch event in Des Essarts. It was the first time that we had tested ourselves together whereas other formations had done a lot of work on the subject but no matter, it was impossible for us with our respective ambitions. We had certainly taken part in the team against-the-clock event of Tirreno, but the team was very different there, especially without Jurgen Van den Broeck. We accomplished the course three times: it was very interesting.'

The Shock of the 'Vansevenant Affair'

The rest was far less amusing. In Belgium, people were speaking only of the Wim Vansevenant affair, retired from the sport but now, on that occasion, the team's driver. The man was at the centre of a police anti-doping investigation. A parcel coming from Australia and intended for him had been intercepted at Zaventem Airport. It contained some 'TB-500', a peptide hormone. Vansevenant told the investigators that it was a question of products intended for his personal use in relation to the animals on his recently acquired farm. But the Press took the affair off in another direction. With its fingers burnt by the Festina affair in 1998 or by the Puerto affair in 2006, each time just a few days before the start of the Tour, it was unable avoid jumping to conclusions, it was logical.

'For us, it was shock and consternation since Vansevenant was a former member of the team. In the bus, Marc Sergeant had brought everyone together. The atmosphere was awful because each of us was wondering whether any one of us was in any way connected with the affair. We were confused, unable to understand. Marc had been quite sure about it, explaining to us that it was perhaps a set-up to disturb us, that we should have more faith in each other, that we shouldn't allow ourselves to be brought down by the comments that were going to follow. It was however all so simple: Vansevenant driver in the team and distributor of products and bingo! I was already imagining already the worst and I saw myself returning home early. The Omega Pharma-Lotto team excluded before the start, for example, for ethical reasons, on suspicion of doping. Fortunately, there was nothing of that. And we still don't know any more about it today.'

'The Thursday is the longest day for the riders. Time passes quickly while waiting for the Tour: you don't have time to be bored. There is the traditional blood test to see whether you are suitable, then the famous presentation of the teams to the public. Before that, we were all assembled in a marquis, riders, sport managers, trainers, mechanics etc, for the organizers' great briefing. Jean-François Pescheux evoked the technical aspects there, such as the order of

the cars, Christian Prudhomme the ethical aspect, very interesting
furthermore, on doping, with no allusion at all to the Vansevenant
affair. His words pleased me: it was not a banal repetition of
platitudes. Then, we awaited our turn in the amphitheatre of the
Puy-du-Fou, after which we left, because enough was enough. On
the Thursday, actually, we're on our feet all the time, which is
"prohibited", if I may say so, for a professional rider. I therefore didn't
hear the whistles of the public with regard to Contador, I had left.'

On the Friday, when the team had hired Nico Mattan to replace
Vansevenant as the VIP driver, Phil was woken very early by some messages.
The Belgian Press was off the leash, it was lumping the affair together with
a possibly organized doping syndrome. *'I had cast an eye on the forums and*
had seen that the "specialists" considered that I could not be achieving such a
season without doping. People were reacting in the same sense, it was wounding,
and I quickly turned off my phones in order to hear no more. I was disgusted. I
had taken my new stopwatch bicycle and I trained on it in order to get used to it
while waiting for the traditional press conference.'

The Vansevenant affair was having, in any case, a snowball effect. The teams'
vehicles were searched, as was even the bag bringing the tricolour jerseys
from Belgium by HST! The Quick Step bus, for a reason that escaped everyone, was dismantled, or almost, by the police of La Roche-sur-Yon where the
other Belgian team was also staying. The atmosphere was noxious, suffocat-
ing. In the overly small room envisaged for the Press in the Mercury Hotel,
the faces were serious. Philippe, Greipel and Van den Broeck were aligned,
narrowly, behind a table in front of a multitude of microphones and cameras.

'Marc Sergeant had asked us not to mention the Vansevenant affair because
there was no reason for so doing, but I didn't listen to him, I was annoyed, I
wanted to give some of them a piece of my mind. That did me good!'

Here, in essence, is what he declared in a tense environment where only the
whirring of the cameras was heard.

'I would like to specify to the newspapers and other media that are lumping together the Vansevenant affair and my performances since the beginning of the season that these allegations have profoundly affected, hurt and disappointed me. But, extremely fortunately, I feel strong enough in my mind to face an event that I know will be testing at the media level. I have too many objectives at the sporting level to be disturbed by these absurd aberrations but I had wanted to say that and also to express some serious doubts about some of your colleagues. Furthermore, if the colour of my hair is of interest to any of you, you should know that it was a question of a bet with my hairdresser if I were to be the champion of Belgium. Is that OK for you?' (Extract from* Le Soir *newspaper of 02 July 2011).

'Afterwards, I had a glass of pink wine with my brother Christian and some friends, despite the presence of the cameras that were continuing to film me. I was finally more relaxed than I thought. I had reccied the arrival until the top of the Mont-des-Alouettes for, although I knew Les Herbiers well, I had never gone right to the top, and that reccy confirmed my idea that this arrival suited me wonderfully. But I knew that I was in the Tour, the greatest cycling event of the year. When you approach a classic, you give your all for a day. In the Tour, that lasts three weeks, so you have to calculate your efforts, and that's not my speciality. I will however have to adapt to it and to proportion my efforts in order to finish in Paris. But nor did I want to ride against my temperament. Nor was I the only candidate for victory at Mont-des-Alouettes. And in addition I had no reference, except a second place in Plumelec in 2008 behind Valverde. But, since that period, I have evolved mentally and physically. I was ready to take up the challenge but I wasn't thinking only of myself. Jurgen Van den Broeck and André Greipel also had their ambitions. And then my season was already successful. I had achieved my goals beyond my hopes. I was there without any pressure, to enjoy myself.'

The 2011 Tour was finally up and running. A considerable crowd had gathered on the island of Noirmoutier.

A Very Violent Effort

'There, in my mind, I reviewed the images of my first Tour, in 2005.
There was a 16-kilometre timed event to open the ball; Armstrong
had already scored a triumph by teaching Ulrich a lesson. For me, it
was a bad memory, I had been mediocre. At the start, the distinctive
jerseys of the champions of various countries were assembled, I was
beside Cancellara and Chavanel, and it was very impressive. At the
briefing, Marc Sergeant's words had been simple: ride in front to
avoid the falls because, he had said, there inevitably would be some.
Jürgen Van den Broeck had to be protected from every problem and
I had to be positioned to win the stage. But the first big fall came
from one of our guys with Van de Walle. There, I thought that it was
a bad start, and that we were losing a top-quality teammate, but
he not only returned but he did a huge amount of work, despite his
injuries. We were well placed when the big fall that had involved
Contador had split the peloton in two at the approach of the arrival.
I hadn't seen it, but I had heard it. We were in a straight line, and
I had turned around in order to assess the situation. Rather than at
180, we were going to fight it out at 70 on the bump, but that didn't
change anything for me. We had to remain in the first positions.
I knew that the first stage of the Tour was spirited but there, you
couldn't believe it. There was even more rubbing than in a classic.
To remain upright, you had to use your elbows. I remember having
touched Boasson-Hagen and Wiggins who were not dawdling, all at
70 kph! In the last kilometres, we were dispersed, I could no longer
see my team mates, things were going too quickly to look because the
end was very technical with tight turns then, at the bottom of the rise,
I had recovered them all, it was the perfect scenario. Even Greipel
was there to toughen the pace even more, it was lovely to see. I knew
that Thomas Voeckler was going to launch an attack; it was logical
and was expected by the entire population of the Vendée! So it didn't
take me by surprise. Vinokourov's attack hurt me more because it was
violent and I know Alex well, when he's on form, he can hurt. Me, I
was on velvet, frankly, with Roelandts and Vanendert who enabled
me to economise until Cancellara's acceleration, which, also, I had

*expected. I returned quickly enough, then he stopped but when I
saw that there had been a pretty pile-up, I no longer had any choice,
and I was obliged to continue at 450 metres from the line. I knew
that there was a yellow jersey at the end. It lasted thirty seconds,
but what pain! My legs hurt, my arms hurt, and I had made a very
violent effort that day. My aches and pains were compensated by
the joy which I experienced little by little, even if I had not got up to
take some seconds from the others because I was thinking, already, of
the possible time loss in the next day's team against-the-clock event!
Then I crossed the line kissing my champion of Belgium jersey. It was
already bringing me joy! I had promised Patricia a yellow jersey for
her birthday, on 02 July, and I had done it!'*

My First Podium of the Tour

At the foot of windmill that spreads its wings on that Vendée hillock, Phil's
supporters were laughing, crying, and screaming their indescribable joy. And
the local public was conquered by the smile of a rider whom it knew well.
The Vendée public likes cycling and appreciates its champions.

*'It was the first time that I had mounted a podium of the Tour De France! Even
in 2005, when I had received the fighting spirit prize after the Champs-Elysées
stage, I had not been on it because on the last day, it's in the regulations; the
fighter of the day is not called on to the podium. For the exploit, I had benefitted by donning three jerseys! I had read the following day in a newspaper,
"Gilbert, the Chameleon", that summarised my situation well since I had taken
the yellow, the polka dot and the green. In the morning, I had told my trainer
Dirk Leenaert to prepare my different coloured watches that I had especially
ordered from Belgium. He seemed flabbergasted when I asked him to have them
ready in his bag for the arrival. I really wanted to. I therefore slipped on a different watch with each jersey. I wanted to enjoy the occasion, which furthermore
greatly amused Gerard Holtz, from France Television, each time I came down
from the podium. Afterwards, I had been stupefied to discover the enormous
media machine. Interviews for France Television, then others for the "entitled"
television channels, which therefore pay in advance to broadcast the Tour, the*

channels without rights, the radio stations, the new media (the Internet) and then the written Press! I had to repeat the same thing twenty times in several languages. I think that it all took about an hour. Add half an hour, minimum, for the anti-doping and the return to the hotel, do the maths. I couldn't give a damn about it, I was so happy but I was tired.'

'That evening, we had obviously drunk some champagne. Herman Frison, my sports manager, had wanted me to "spray" the bottle. As a result, I put some of it everywhere but it was especially he who tasted it: he was soaked but hadn't he wanted it? I had been a bit of a vandal, in a way, but what you want; we're all still kids, quickly content with idiotic japes. When I returned to my room that I was sharing with Jelle Vanendert, the other riders and the members of staff all wanted to touch the yellow jersey. I had installed it on a chair between the two beds, and we all looked at it as though it was a present under a Christmas tree. When I was young, the jersey of which I dreamed the most was the world cup one. When I saw Bartoli and Vandenbroucke with it, it made me want it, but unfortunately, that world cup of the classics no longer exists, which is a pity for me! On the subject of dreams, I quickly fell asleep; I have an ability to switch off pretty quickly and to think of the next day's stage. I hardly looked at the messages on my phones, they were too numerous, I couldn't decently answer everyone. And I take this opportunity of thanking all of you to whom I had failed to reply!'

CHAPTER 19

My Birthday, An Unhappy Memory

While Phil and Jelle were resting in La Roche-sur-Yon, not far from there, in Saint-March-la-Réorthe at the place called the Bas Pouët, an unusual atmosphere was animating that peaceful place. *'That's the guest house where I go to stay each time with Olivier Kaisen for the against-the-clock of Les Herbiers. The owner, Joseph Briand, is a seasoned cyclist, a Kaisen family friend. He has cycled all around Japan all on his own - well done ! We've became friends.'* Joseph and his wife Isabelle had only one dream on the morning of the first stage: to see Philippe in yellow. With their usual discretion, they were content to send him a text, while in the gite, Christian and several of Phil's supporters were celebrating the victory, accompanied in particular by Michel, the former slater from Burkina Faso, who used to operate on the Tour on his motor bike in his yellow boiler suit and whose laughter resounded to the stars which dominated the sky of the Vendée and Philippe Gilbert's dreams.

> *'On the subject of motor bikes, it should be known that until recently, the organisation of the Tour sent the results to the hotel, as well as a set of distinctive jerseys for the runners concerned. However, for reasons of economy and ecology combined, all that is finished: the results are available on the Internet: they just have to be consulted. As for the jerseys, they are distributed at the OPP (Obligatory Points of Passage) when one goes to the start. However, I very much wanted to have the yellow jersey for going to train with the team next morning. It was legitimate ! I had rung Jean-François Pescheux, the Tour's Competitions Director, and he granted me that favour: fifteen minutes later, a motorcyclist arrived at the hotel with the jersey. When we took our dispositions for the warm-up at the foot of the Omega Pharma-Lotto bus, a broad safety area had been established, much broader than usual. I had understood why: there was an enormous crowd: I was the impact which the possession of the jersey represented for people and I was pretty proud !'*

My friend Hushovd comes first

Garmin, BMC, Leopard: there were some fine people for ogling Philippe's jersey. The timed team event was not the Belgian formation's speciality, nor can everything be expected of it. *'We knew that we were going to lose the jersey before leaving, the gaps were too small but, in my heart of hearts, I firmly believed in it. We were fairly relaxed, that was an advantage I find, on the starting grid, impressive, where the crowd applauded. But that relaxation was not transformed into concentration. We left too much slowly whereas we could have gone more quickly and, unfortunately, our sports manager never shouted into the earpiece that we had to accelerate. We fell asleep, there's no other expression, and at the first intermediate check point, when we had all upped the pace, it was already too late, and we never recovered a place, furthermore. I knew, as we went along, that I had lost my yellow jersey but I had savoured it, I had so much hoped for it that I had no regrets.'*

As envisaged, the battle raged, in Des Essarts, between Garmin and the BMC, and at the end of some remarkable suspense, it was Thor Hushovd, Philippe's training friend, who donned the yellow jersey. The American team had designated the world champion in the event of a collective victory. *'The fact that Thor had taken the yellow tunic had softened my disappointment and then let's not forget that I was nevertheless on the podium, that I still had the green jersey and that of the best uphiller. It was Cadel Evans who was wearing the green in the race that day because when a rider takes all the jerseys, as I had done at Mont-des-Alouettes, the other tunics are worn by the second, third, etc. I was therefore able to join Thor on the podium, and I could see that he was happy. After the protocol, the Press etc, I returned by bike because there were traffic jams everywhere. I was dressed as the champion of Belgium and everyone recognised me, it was impressive. I was applauded, when I passed a car, people opened their windows to take photos. I had even passed the RTBF's car and I had time to discuss with Rodrigo Beenkens and Cédric Vasseur, his consultant. I can still remember the place: it was on the secondary road 160!'*

On 04 July, the Tour left the Vendée by the Sables d'Olonne heading for Redon, a red-letter stage for the sprinters. *'Our mission was to take Greipel along for the sprint: that was the watchword. Everyone was asking me, on the morning at the start, if it wasn't complicated for me to do the work for André, due to the fact that I was wearing the green jersey, but I've never made any mystery of my intentions in relation to that tunic, it didn't seem to me to be a priority, and I was targeting a second stage victory as soon as possible. I had taken Greipel along at the time of the intermediary sprint, he took some points, but behind the breakaway group, that didn't mean much.'*

In that intermediary sprint, the images were conclusive: Thor Hushovd and Mark Cavendish were seriously rubbing each other. On the basis of the video, they were furthermore to be displaced from that sprint after the arrival, which had not made the world champion and the yellow jersey wearer lose his smile as he explained: *'I had simply wanted to put a little sun lotion on Cavendish's forearm!'*

That made everyone laugh but not the Englishman, down in the dumps, who surprised everyone, including Romain Feillu, whom he designated as the culprit of his failed sprint. And thoroughly failed furthermore since Rojas too had got the better of him. Rojas, the champion of Spain, a man who, although Phil was unaware of it at that time, was going to annoy him in this Tour. Because he, contrary to Phil, was aiming at the green jersey and was convinced that his rival was too. Cavendish's bad mood was fortunately replaced by the broad smile of the winner, Tyler Farrar, who had had time to designate with the fingers of his two hands the 'W' of Wouter, the Christian name of his deceased friend. The American had promised Weylandt's father that he would win a stage on the Tour, and he had. It was also the first stage victory on the Grande Boucle for the man from Ghent by adoption.

'Bad feelings at the massage'

'The transfer to the hotel, after the arrival, was long. I had again mounted on the podium because although I had lost the green jersey this time to Rojas, I still had the polka dot tunic! When I had arrived on the massage table in Dirk Leenaert's hands, I felt that my legs were not OK. It hadn't taken Dirk long to confirm it. There was no explanation, if not the hours of tiredness off the bike with the

protocol obligations, the Press, and the anti-doping procedures. A lot of energy is wasted in all that. When it is said that the great leaders to everything they can to avoid taking jerseys too early in the event, it is the truth, and it's to avoid all that ceremonial, which is extremely nervously exhausting. In short, on the day before my birthday things were not great, and in the morning, waking up on my 29th *birthday in Lorient, they weren't any better. Moreover, it was raining!'*

The local, national and international press however held their front pages that day, with a photograph of Phil and Thor side by side with this caption: *'Will Gilbert regain the yellow jersey from his friend Hushovd at the top of Mûr-de-Bretagne?'* As much to say that an enormous pressure was weighing on Philippe's shoulders, but he had got used to it !

'Jelle hurts me !'

'The never-ending rain complicated things, especially as I was not happy about my legs. In front, the breakaway groups were being elastic: ensuring the pursuit wasn't easy. My team mates had worked all the time, and then we finally received a helping hand, from the BMC team. I knew that Mûr-de-Bretagne rise; I had already taken it with the Tour in 2008. It didn't suit me, especially because it is so rectilinear and severe that every move can be seen from afar. No question, there, of surprising somebody on a bend ! As soon as we joined the breakaway group, the motivation returned. Legs or not, there I was driven by morale, I thought that success was possible, and then it was my birthday all the same ! At 1,500 metres from the top, I reckoned that Jelle Vanendert was in stunning condition. He had had brought one hell of a pace and I had been unable to follow him: he hurt me very badly but he couldn't have known it. I had however yelled for him to slow down but he didn't hear me. I was in an impossible position: if I let Jelle go, the others would think that I wasn't strong enough and I would be countered; or I would be overdrawn *(typical expression in cycling which means exceeding ones threshold of resistance). It was at that particular moment that*

the race was amplified to an extent that exceeded the context of the simple stage victory. The heavyweights came on scene where they were not expected. Contador put in a sharp acceleration, I was obliged to go behind even though I was already "flat out". The Spaniard had every reason to attack because Andy Schleck wasn't there, he had lost time during the first stage, so each second that he could make up was a bonus, no matter where. It was hard with the wind, Contador, as a pure uphiller, slowed down then started again, that hurt me very badly especially when Cadel Evans joined in the debate. Because the context of this stage was quickly forgotten: Hushovd had a slight lead on Cadel in the general classification, his yellow jersey was threatened but I had said myself that it wasn't urgent, for BMC, to take the tunic already. Everything in fact was against me: the rain, my less rare legs, the leaders who were waging war.'

'The false argument with Jurgen'

'When Van den Broeck had attacked on the left, I had initially let him do so, then I jumped on to his wheel, which gave me a launching pad. I was mistaken: it was especially helpful to Evans and Contador. Cadel had won a stage of the same kind in the Tirreno by launching the sprint from afar. It was furthermore on that particular day that I understood that he was very strong in this Tour. There was immediately a raging argument on the fact that I had ridden behind Jürgen. At the briefing, there had never been any question that he would attack. I had therefore regarded his manœuvre as a tactic to help me, and if he had wanted to win the stage, he should have spoken about it beforehand. It was not the plan and one habitually respects the initial tactic in the team. We did not evoke this argument at the arrival in front of the journalists. In the bus, there was tension, very perceptible tension. When we got to the hotel, Marc Sergeant asked us to remain in the bus in order to discuss things calmly. One hour after the arrival, it was better, especially for me, as I can sometimes be impulsive. Jürgen had explained that he was feeling good, that he had left on that feeling and me, as I said, that I had the feeling that *his attack was intended to take me along. In any case, we were fully agreed about one thing: neither he nor I would have been able to beat Evans or Contador. Even though after the arrival, Cadel had admitted to me that he was convinced that I was going to overtake him again when he had attacked. He hadn't expected to win!'*

To such an extent that at the moment of crossing the line, it was Alberto Contador who was convinced of his victory because he had raised his arms. The most surprised, in the story, was Thor Hushovd, who had succeeded in keeping up with the pure uphillers in order to keep his yellow jersey, which made him say at the arrival: '*It's thanks to Philippe if I have produced the finest athletic performance of my career in the Tour because he has forced me, in training, to do some sprints on the bumps. I've often suffered from that, but this time, I can thank him!'*

Finally at the hotel, Phil had found his champion of Belgium jersey again, like Cinderalla with neither shoe nor coach after the ball. '*Mine was a little spoiled, I was furious with myself, I had the feeling of having ridden badly. Dirk Leenaert's massage and remarks had enabled me to relativise, to turn the page, once again, and to think of the following day.*'

CHAPTER 20

Second at Cap Frehel and Super Besse

It never rains in Brittany, the Bretons will always tell you, but whenever you go there, it's raining. Odd, isn't it? On the morning of 06 July, the clemency of the sky was however entirely real, but the wind was gusting. With a stage that skirts the Côtes d'Armor, permanent pitfalls on the narrow roads were guaranteed. The leaders had been warned: the day towards the splendid Cap Fréhel would not be simple. *'When I was on the podium at Mont-des-Alouettes, the deputy mayor of Cap Fréhel was also there. He had had time to explain to me why this arrival was made for me and had advised me to ride in front!'* That was judicious because, in the peloton, it was war. Some, inattentive, went off in a nosedive, and not the least important: Boonen, Gesink, Wiggins, Contador, Brajkovic, to mention only them, found themselves on the asphalt with their shorts in tatters, the grimaces on their faces expressing pain and frustration in equal measure. *'At the briefing, Greipel had expressed a desire to win, so the message was clear for everyone. After the Saint-Brieuc crossing, the course was rather technical, one could quickly lose ground on a bend or a bump. I had even had to push Greipel on one of them. Voeckler had tried on his own, as he knows how, but the HTC were already in place, organized around Cavendish with Tony Martin at the head of the group, and that was hurting everyone. I had remained calmly on their wheels until the moment when, as I came out of three or four bends, a door opened in front of me without my having to brake. My bicycle was leaning over as far as possible like a GP motor bike, and I was doing 75 kph. There, I no longer turned around, I charged, I imagined that Greipel was on my wheel but I didn't see him. When the sprint was launched, I pulled out and I took my chance. If nobody touched my rear wheel, I would win, it was certain.'* But it was Cavendish who swooped first. The devil from the Isle of Man had had to tear himself away in order to beat Phil. *'He told me after the race that that sprint had been the most difficult of his life.'* And he confirmed it to the Press, adding that it was his

finest since his victory in San Remo ahead of Haussler. After having therefore made the race with Evans, Contador and the uphillers the day before,
Gilbert was now competing with the finest sprinters: that is called eclecti-
cism ! *I never like to be second but behind Cavendish in a massive sprint, the
disappointment is easier to digest !'*

'I wanted to give up the Tour !'

As a result, Phil took the green jersey again and found the joys and
the obligations of the protocol once again. When he returned to
the bus, his good mood was quickly curtailed. *I went up into the
bus and when I passed in front of Greipel, he turned his head away,
I could see that he was avoiding me. Then he exploded: he accused
me of boxing him in. I didn't understand. At the same moment,
Eurosport was rebroadcasting the images of the arrival, and I
benefited from them to ask him where, frankly, I could have boxed
him in. He looked but he stuck to his guns, and then he yelled: "You
are an egoist, you always ride for yourself, you never do anything
for the others." Marc Sergeant was not present at the time of this
quarrel. I sent Greipel packing and then I went to take my shower.
When Sergeant arrived, I told him that I was not going to start the
following day. I couldn't accept Greipel's insinuations and, since it
was like that, he had to only manage without me. After all, my Tour
had been successful: I had had all the jerseys, I could go home ! Yes,
I was angry, extremely angry ! My departure would have been more
of a problem for the sponsor than for me. Nobody, up to that point,
had spoken to me like that, and in addition, Greipel didn't listen
to what was said to him: he spoke, he yelled. The atmosphere was
so hateful in the bus that the majority returned to the hotel by car.
Sergeant hadn't liked it. When he arrived at the hotel, he interrupted
the massages and sent everyone into the bus for a hefty debriefing.
Marc gave his version but André didn't let up: he repeated that I was
an individualist. I had answered that I had had an extraordinary
opportunity in the final sprint and that I was not going to brake all
the same ! I had then explained that when somebody was pushing*

him on the bumps because he wasn't keeping up, it was me! Things then calmed down, we went off to eat after a somewhat flaccid handshake. Greipel was also undoubtedly frustrated because he had been unable to pit himself against his sworn enemy, Cavendish. Afterwards, during the meal, I learned that on arriving, he had thrown his bicycle against the bus and had said in front of the TV cameras: "This team isn't a team." You can imagine the atmosphere. On my side, I had obviously retracted my decision to withdraw...'

The following day, the Belgian Press evoked the Gilbert-Greipel affair at length. It had surmised in any case that there was a problem because, as far as the bus was concerned, in Cap Fréhel, it had remained desperately closed for the Press and no press release had been issued by e-mail. In his daily column that he held as consultant for the 'Le Soir' newspaper, Eddy Merckx put forward a pertinent analysis. *'At the beginning, Omega Pharma-Lotto had chosen to work on three tableaux: Gilbert, Van den Broeck and Greipel. It is very complicated to have so many objectives in a Tour De France. Then, I think that the announcement of the future separation of the two sponsors can't have helped the atmosphere because the riders are inevitably being coveted elsewhere.'*

'Free hand for Vanendert at Lisieux'

'Personally, I didn't concern myself with all that: I was in the Tour, full stop. I had the green jersey, a problem with Greipel that I had forgotten on the morning of the Dinan stages where, as on the two previous days, it was raining. As regards the road, the Lisieux arrival suited me, once again. Undoubtedly because of the rain, I didn't have the legs of the previous day, but the same unpleasant feelings as the other day. One had to be attentive that day, the roads were slippery and dangerous, but in the team, we had refound our spirits. We even rode well, often in front, because before ascending the hill of the basilica of Lisieux, there was a wicked right-angle bend that had to be negotiated to perfection. Contrary to the other days, I had chosen to hold myself back while waiting to see what would happen. I had said to Jelle that if it wanted to go, he shouldn't hesitate, and that is

what he did. He left rather early on the bump, everyone was looking at thinking that it was for me to make a tempo but I didn't move, on the contrary.'

Behind, Contador in person, who seemed decidedly more and more at ease in the rain, started the chase, and then it was the turn of the stubborn Voeckler, who had a go, as he did each day. The Alsatian caught up with Vanendert at the 1,500-metre panel but Jelle, logically, didn't take over. An ideal situation for Philippe when everything was grouped together under the red flame under the impetus, in particular, of the Sky team?

'No, on that particular day, I was really transparent. Greipel was not there for the sprint either, and as Gerraint Thomas took along Boasson Hagen, there was strictly nothing to do, I was boxed in, he had nothing to say and the ascent had not been as hard as had been thought, there were more than fifty of us to contest the sprint.' The young Boasson beat the 'old' Hushovd, and Lisieux was suddenly transformed into a championship of Norway!

Phil kept his green jersey while the Tour descended towards Chateauroux via Le Mans. *'I call that "Day 7", the most difficult point for me as I'm used to one-week races. The legs start to hurt, the body is exposed to difficult conditions. At the briefing, only one message: everything for Greipel. And I did everything for him. I was in good faith when I ensured him of my participation. However, I hadn't wanted to be the last element of the train in the package: I believed that Roelandts and Sieberg were better armed than me to make the final pass, as one says in football. And that is what occurred. An aside, moreover, on Sieberg. He is an important and very meticulous rider. Each day, thanks to a programme that he has in his computer, he shows us the last kilometres as if the course had been flown over by a helicopter. It is very interesting, especially when a massive sprint is being viewed. I had produced an enormous effort, for a whole kilometre, thoroughly, in order to protect Greipel from the wind. The German had produced a superb sprint, but Cavendish had been even stronger. There was nothing to say. Greipel had immediately thanked the entire team for the work that had been accomplished because we had nothing to reproach ourselves about. That collective clarification did everyone a power of good.'*

'My derailleur gives out in Super Besse'

There were smiles again in the Omega Pharma-Lotto bus. On the other hand, elsewhere, it was grimace soup. Tom Boonen, still suffering from his first fall, gave up, but the news of the day was above all the withdrawal of Bradley Wiggins after a fall. The winner of the Dauphiné was a potential favourite, and now he was gone. On that particular day, Team Sky had made Boasson Hagen wait so that he could possibly help his leader to return. A huge coaching blunder since the Norwegian was still eighth in the classification before the departure from Le Mans and a potential green jersey !

The rain seemed to have been definitively invited to the Tour. The summer was decidedly gloomy. Although you wouldn't think so, the first week had caused some damage. Contador delayed on the first day, Wiggins out of the race, not to mention many other falls: it was therefore with anxious eyes that the riders observed the sky of Aigurande, on the Saturday morning, in order to involve themselves in what should be called the first stage of medium mountains. Because at the end of the course, in the middle of the Auvergne Lakes created millions of years ago by extinct volcanoes, it was the ascent towards the Super Besse station that had left a bad memory for the organizers, with the victory of a certain Ricco.

'As far as my legs were concerned, it wasn't yet exactly what I wanted but it was distinctly better nevertheless. The stage was hard and, once again, our team had assumed practically all the pursuit behind the breakaway group. I got the cherry again by being protected and when we arrived at the final rise, which from afar resembles Mûr-de-Bretagne a little, I was in an ideal situation with Vanendert and Van den Broeck as protection. But, in front, there was an escapee from the breakaway group, the Portuguese Rui Costa, and a man who left like a devil in a counter-attack, Alexandre Vinokourov, a long time virtual yellow jersey. Alex had been caught and I accelerated: I was feeling good. On my wheel, there were Contador, Evans and Andy Schleck, it was a repeat of what had happened at Mûr-de-Bretagne ! Afterwards, I had temporised, I passed over the little plateau again to have a breather, I felt that the leaders wanted to *confront each other but me, I couldn't have cared less, I needed the stage victory and Costa was still in front. When I wanted to give the great development, the derailleur didn't obey my orders I could no longer attack, but only follow. I had undoubtedly lost some precious seconds until the moment when the large plateau was passed by again. There, I got everyone away from my wheels but I failed by a few seconds behind Costa. I was very disappointed because, tactically, we hadn't made any mistake. Once again, I had been betrayed by my equipment. I recovered, however, the green jersey, because Rojas was far, but I wanted to win my second stage, but I failed. Second at Cap Fréhel, second at Super Besse, I counted the opportunities that slipped under my nose but, in the Tour, everything is more difficult, and one has to live with that reality. In addition, nothing is ever wasted: by accumulating my places, I was taking points for the World Tour classification. They'll count later!'*

CHAPTER 21

Van den Broeck's Fall

The organizers had hoped for a lot from the weekend in Auvergne. The hilly region offered, on paper, some splendid jousts including that of Super Besse, where the big names were honing their motivations as the fire smouldering under the volcanoes promised much for Saint-Flour. Philippe, for his part, had captured everyone's attention at the Issoire start. Winner of the first stage, second in two stages, able to rub with sprinters and climbers, Phil was also considerably annoying the candidates for the green jersey, Rojas in particular, who was seeing him everywhere. How far was he going to go, people were wondering? Up to where could he climb when the passes would be sharper, longer, and steeper?

Hell in the Pas de Peyrol

'On the Sunday, in Issoire, I had legs of fire. I had got over the seven-day hurdle and I felt the same as I had on the morning of the first day. Like everyone, I had cast an attentive eye on the course and on those tortuous roads without practically a single yard of flat on the way to Saint-Flour. That suited me perfectly. The idea wasn't to defend my green jersey, but to win. A green jersey, however, is not allowed to leave in a breakaway group and, on that day, Voeckler had brought his warriors with him, such as Flecha, Hoogerland, Luis-Leon Sanchez: everyone remembers it. A superb breakaway group, well constructed, with for each the will to go to the end, to take turns, to take who knows, for one or other of them, the yellow jersey. The breakaway group had a big lead and, in the Omega Pharma-Lotto team, we decided to manage the pursuit fairly early because in a stage like that one, a peloton can makes up for lost time with difficulty and slowly. The Garmins of Thor Hushovd, who had however virtually lost his yellow jersey, didn't seem terribly keen to work with us, and that had annoyed me. There had just been Julian Dean in front who had undertaken the descent of the Pas de Peyrol pass at the head of the peloton. The descent was technical, and the road was slippery. Dean followed the motor bike that was in front of him. Suddenly, we took a wet turn, from left to right. A turn like so much of others except that this one is "blind", it is suddenly closed and nothing can any longer can be seen. Before seeing the fall, I had heard it. An incredible crash of bicycles and riders strewn all over the place. I had seen Vinokourov going straight into a hole, a ditch or a ravine, I didn't yet know. I concentrated on my path, I took the inside, my old cyclo-cross reflexes, there again, had come to my aid. I had vaguely seen, in a flash, that two of our riders were involved in the fall. I quickly knew that it was a question of Van den Broeck then Willems. There, I put myself at the head of the peloton in order to obstruct, because as long as there was no information, I believed that it would not have been normal to ride. I had somewhat assumed Cancellara's role, the one that he had played in the Spa in 2010 after the collective fall in Stavelot. But here, it was above all while waiting for news because, I repeat, I had legs of fire, the breakaway obviously took advantage of the circumstances to take a lead again but no matter, I had to know. I had no news via the earpiece because Frison and Sergeant had logically left their car. I was anxious, especially for Willems, because some in the peloton were saying that he hadn't got back up from the ditch.'

'When you no longer have any information the earpiece, it's difficult to receive any, which is why, as I've said in a previous chapter, I've changed mind on this subject. Because I had yelled several times to draw the attention of one of the organisation's motorcyclists, who didn't seem to understand that I wanted information. When he had finally twigged, we were at the top of the next pass. I knew that Jürgen had not set out again and, especially, that Willems was in hospital. We were deprived of two new pawns, one of whom was a potential winner of the final ranking, after having lost Van de Walle earlier in the Tour. I was unhappy for Jürgen because we were founding great hopes on him. We had up to that point run a perfect race by protecting him; he could approach the mountain without having wasted time on the other favourites: it was sad for him.'

'When we resumed, I had been able to catch up with the breakaway group all the same. There was still a way to accomplish something. Curiously, in our ranks, Sebastian Lang made me understand that he didn't want to ! With Vanendert and Roelandts, we got going again but it was difficult to have the assistance of the other teams. We had found Dean again, who had stopped to spend a penny after having realised that, if he was all alone in front, it was because there had been a problem upstream, and then when I saw one of the organisation's cars in the distance with a rider behind it, that bucked up my spirits once again. I said to myself that it was perhaps still possible to get into it. When we had passed Juan-Antonio Flecha, he was in tatters; I wondered what he had done to be in such a state. My surprise was even greater when we had caught up Hoogerland, whose legs were lacerated and bleeding. We had received no information about that accident between the Press car and the breakaway group riders. We had learned about it from Flecha, who had had the information passed along the entire peloton before being left by it.'

Images that had gone around the world when a television car, driving fast to take some cassettes back to the arrival, ran into the riders who were in front. Of the five members of the breakaway group, Flecha and Hoogerland were the hardest hit, but it was a miracle. For the same price, they could all have fallen, or even have paid with their lives. A scandal which, in the unanimous opinion of the followers, was not sufficiently reprimanded, that evening, in Saint-Flour.

'Abandoned by my derailleur'

'In front, there was still no wild desire from the Garmins or the BMCs to ride. But I still believed it when, in a rather technical descent which called for even more attention since the recent fall, my chain got blocked. Impossible to pedal even though the last hill was awaiting us. I had raised my hand as high as possible but I imagined that a quick repair would be difficult on a descent where the peloton was in single file. It was furthermore dangerous: I was being passed by guys at full speed, I was for them an obstacle, a moving traffic island, and I was really afraid that they would crash into me. When the car finally arrived, I was on the left-hand side of the road, and I immediately crossed over to go and find my bicycle that was supposed to be on the right-hand side of the gallery. This is an interesting detail: on the roof of the cars, there are usually four bicycles: those on the right, the first and the last, belong to the leaders. I therefore knew immediately that mine was on the right, except that the mechanic had made *a mistake and had placed it on the left. And bingo, a further waste of time for little things that cost you energy, irritation and nervous impulse. Roelandts had waited for me on the Château d'Alleuze hill where I zigzagged between all the stragglers, then Jelle took me along, he had incredible strength and so did I, but we knew that we were done for. The gap with the leading group was definitive, but all the same I made it a point of honour to go and get the fourth place. I remember having displayed my disappointment when crossing the line, because I was convinced to have let slip a stage victory which, because of my incredible legs, would have been duly done and dusted. But what could my disappointment be compared to the falls and the dramas experienced by others?'*

That day propelled Thomas Voeckler into the yellow and Vinokourov, who was within an inch of claiming the leader's tunic the day before, into hell. Wound up by his team mates like a disjointed puppet, the Kazakh had undoubtedly, on that Pas de Peyrol, drawn a line on his career.

'When Marc Sergeant brought us together, he gave us some reassuring news of Willems and Van den Broeck. There were only six of us left: he lifted our spirits. "The Tour is still long", he had said, "we still have some objectives". Oddly, when we found ourselves at six, there was more closeness between us. In the bus, we sat down together rather than taking advantage of the space logically and unfortunately left by the three who had scratched.'

As a result, the green jersey that had not been an objective for the Belgian team at the beginning of the Tour became one as circumstances dictated, even though, with six riders, the bet would be difficult. Although Gilbert had increased his lead over Cavendish, and over Rojas, whose difficulties had been discernible when the road rose, it would still be necessary to get back to work because while the Englishman could be patient while waiting for the potential mass arrivals, Gilbert would have to anticipate. And in the debate, one should not overlook the chances of Evans who, although preoccupied by another, yellower, objective, had shown himself to be entirely legitimate since the beginning of the hostilities.

'I had become leader of my formation on the Tour for a day, but I wasn't therefore focusing on the green jersey: it was too blurred for me. My priority, right

then, was to think of those who were suffering from the after-effects of the fall, of the fact that their season was over. As soon as I could, I communicated with Vinokourov on his hospital bed, and I was glad to know that he was in good hands. We were also in a hurry to benefit, in Saint-Flour, from our first day of rest.'

'When are you giving up, Jelle?'

'On the Monday, we had ridden for more or less ninety minutes, I had donned the champion of Belgium jersey, not the green one. In a village, we had stopped to drink a couple of beers in a bar. To decompress, that does a crazy amount of good. People don't always understand that: when they see a high-level sports-man drinking alcohol, they think it's indecent, and I've never understood why. Two little beers, they do you good, believe me, after ten days of permanent tension. Afterwards, I met the Press at the hotel, the atmosphere was decidedly more relaxed than at the beginning of Tour, and there were fewer journalists too. We also made a detour via the private clinic to go and say hello to Jürgen. All that had been decided privately and in secret, but there were however cameras waiting for us on the clinic's car park. I sometimes have the feeling of being a fairground animal: it's irritating. It was the first time of my life that I had met Jurgen Van den Broeck's parents, although I had been riding beside him since 1998. His girlfriend was there too, and our visit pleased him. He had already turned the page, he spoke about Vuelta. I have already said, I think, but there were means of getting on to the podium in Paris, undoubtedly not to beat Evans, but he had everything he needed to make a big success of the Tour. Therefore you should always take advantage of the moments that happen when you are in form and being successful. We also had another secret weapon: Jelle Vanendert. Jelle shared my room each night and each day, my joke was the same: "So, Jelle, when are you giving up?" I used to tease him with that because, up to that point, he hadn't yet finished a Tour. By saying that to him, I knew that I was motivating him even more. However, I knew and I could see that he had exceptional legs, and that he had never displayed such form on a Tour.'

CHAPTER 22

'Jelle's Plateau'

The Tour De France was resumed from Aurillac, on the Tuesday, still shaken by the Sunday's events. The accident caused by the Press car had put the entire caravan into a bad mood. A delicate tension between the followers and the organizers was felt. In terms of the sport, this Tour had also been decapitated: Van den Broeck, Wiggins and Vinokourov had gone, and Gesink was known not to be A1, that made nevertheless four weighty outsiders who would no longer join the fray that was supposedly being run by the Schleck brothers, Evans and Contador. At his press conference, Philippe had acknowledged for the first time that the green jersey had become an objective but, in reality, he knew that it would be complicated.

'The race had also changed its physiognomy, let's not forget. Europcar had the yellow jersey with Voeckler but, intelligently, the French team often decided not to conduct the pursuit because we were entering a portion that favoured the sprinters. It was for the HTC, Garmin and those who had not yet won to conduct the pursuit behind the breakaway group. In our team, now six, we no longer had those means but we had a double plan. We had seen on the graph that the hill that was 15 kilometres away from the arrival and could enable us to eliminate the sprinters. This is why we had set the pace on the bump. In my earpiece, I was told that Cavendish was no longer in the peloton, but I was wary all the same. I had continued because the course was lending itself to it. I had the right to attack; it was envisaged in the deal, and at the same time to try my luck, but also to exhaust Greipel's adversaries. Voeckler had jumped into my slipstream, and even now, I haven't understood why. I hadn't constituted a threat for him: I was five minutes behind. Perhaps he had wanted to widen the gap on his opponents? I don't know. Moreover, I hit a snag, a 700-metre hill at four kilometres from the arrival that was not detailed in the road book. I could no longer

continue on my own: I was given relief so that I could recover. My mission, then, was to ride behind Greipel in order to prevent anyone from catching up with him. Thereafter, Sieberg had done the rest. His work was impressive.'

Greipel's Day of Glory

For although the pace imposed by Philippe had not eliminated Cavendish, it had hurt the latter's team mates. The Englishman was on his own in the last kilometre where Sieberg was setting a great pace before being curiously relayed by Oss (Liquigas), who was literally taking Cavendish along towards the victory. However, with an indescribable rage, and a motivation sharpened by Laguiole's knife, Greipel was the first to breast the tape ahead of his sworn enemy. A clear and faultless victory that allowed Philippe, in the peloton, to raise his right arm in salute of his teammate's success. At six, Omega Pharma-Lotto had quickly restored their morale, and had proved the accuracy of Marc Sergeant's remarks, who had insisted that this Tour was not prematurely over.

'On the other hand, but I didn't yet know it, it was the last day on which I was to wear the green jersey. Some have reproached me for attacking from so far on that hill: but it was in the plan, we had respected it to the letter. Greipel was really happy, the team also, and that's what counted. If I hadn't attacked, perhaps Cavendish would have flown over the sprint and I would have lost the green jersey anyway. I train practically every day with Hushovd. He talks, as I do, of his successes, of various races, etc. He has twice won the final green jersey classification in Paris but he never talks about it! I'm not certain that that objective is of major importance in a season. A true sprinter likes to win stages, and also the classics. The green jersey or any similar ranking in other events is seldom mentioned in the history of cycling. On the subject of the stage leading to Lavaur, the following day, I have nothing to say, except that it was appallingly monotonous and that the weather was filthy. We knew that Cavendish would continue with his festivities: it was practically written.'

The sky was so low that July could have been confused with March. Impossible to distinguish, in the distance, the Pyrenees that the riders were impatiently awaiting. The followers and the public, also, were impatient because the first high-mountain stage was becoming indispensable for enabling the big names to reveal themselves. The whole of France, for its part, had only one obsession on that 14 July leading from Cagnaux to Luz-Ardiden: to know whether their hero, Thomas Voeckler, would keep his yellow jersey. During the night, the weather finally changed. It wasn't high summer but it was no longer raining. 'Like everyone, I was fearful of that first mountain stage but, on the contrary, it pleased me well. On the Tourmalet pass, with my pace set by the peloton behind the breakaway group, I had been able to follow and then, in the descent, I had charged, I wanted to have some fun but especially to take Jelle Vanendert along with me. Jelle knows that he can follow me with his eyes closed in a descent: he trusts me.'

The statistics would show it later: it was Phil who had proved to be the fastest in the descent from the Tourmalet. After having sprinted against Cavendish then Contador, here he was again in a new manifestation: that of down-hiller! 'When we arrived at the foot of Luz-Ardiden, I quickly found myself overdrawn, the descent had finished me but Jelle was well placed with Samuel Sanchez, who was however terribly strong that day, it was evident.' Sanchez and Vanendert, an improbable duel, whereas behind, the favourites were play-ing, but too late, their trumps: the Schleck brothers, Frank in particular, had attacked and, in the band, it was Contador who was showing signs of ques-tionable form, the only one in any case who lost time in Luz-Ardiden where the Olympic champion had got ahead of the valiant Vanendert. 'Jelle had tried to leave on his own because he knew that he would be beaten in the sprint. I was disappointed for him but content and proud at the same time that he had been able to shine in such a way in a great mountain stage.'

The Basques were content and shouted their joy (whereas Sanchez, it should be specified, even though he was riding for Euskaltel, is Asturian and not Basque) and the French were too when, taken along by Pierre Roland, Thomas Voeckler saved his yellow jersey.

'The following day, the presence of the Aubisque at 60 kilometres from the arrival towards Lourdes did not plead in favour of a fight between

*the great. I had very much wanted to leave in the breakaway group, it
was a thing for me, but neither the HTC team of Cavendish nor the
Movistar team of Rojas were allowing me the slightest opportunity.
That green jersey still had me marked, it was really irritating. I had
always had either Martin, or Eisel on my wheel but OK, that was
the name of the game. In that kind of situation, I just waited to see
what would happen. Jelle took some points for the polka dot jersey but
I quickly understood, in front, that the breakaway group had left for
good and that nothing was going to happen between the favourites
during that stage.'*

Left behind on the Aubisque by better climbers than he, such as Jérémy Roy
(who had already crossed the Tourmalet in the lead all alone the day before)
and David Moncoutié, Hushovd however returned in the descent then on the
plain before successively disposing of the Frenchmen in a pretty impressive
number. *'I was happy for him, and proud too. I imagined his joy of winning with
the world champion jersey. I waited until 22:00 before calling him: I knew that he
would be quietly in his room at that time. At that particular moment, neither of
us had yet chosen to link our fate with that of BMC.'* The following day, the greatest stage of the Pyrenees was on the menu. The Beille Plateau, which was awaiting the riders, has a particular destiny because with each time it has accommodated the Tour, it has received the future winner there: Pantani, Armstrong
and Contador have all won up there and then finished in yellow in Paris.

'I had tears in my eyes'

*'The rain had given way, suddenly, to some intense heat. In the
peloton, it was a race for the water bottles. Getting supplied was
difficult and I remember a moment when I had been very thirsty. I
would have given 100 euros for a little bottle of water. At one moment,
Flecha came level with me in a descent and he gave me a 33-cl bottle:
he had measured my disarray. It was a gesture that I will never forget
because I was on the verge of dehydration. On that particular day,
Roelandts and Vanendert were on really top form. They impressed
me. I knew however that there would be a brawl between the greats,*

at least I supposed so. In the Port of Lers, Jelle was less good, then, in the following valley, whereas Cancellara went flat out for the Schleck brothers, I had given all that I could with Jürgen Roelandts to bring Jelle at the foot of the Beille Plateau where I was immediately on the road to ruin, I could do no more. The rest I had imagined without seeing anything. Via the information that I was hearing from the Radio Tour motorbikes, I knew that Jelle had had a good finish, once again with Sanchez. Then, when you lose ground in a race, there's no longer any motorbike and therefore no more information. At three kilometres from the arrival, I had come alongside the car of a sports manager, I don't remember which one, who told me of Jelle's victory. The other riders didn't believe it: they laughed. Me, I was so happy that I pressed on the pedals to finish at full speed in order not to miss the protocol ceremony and to see him on the podium, but I didn't get there in time.' 'At the 500-metre panel, I heard the voice of Daniel Mangeas who was proposing applause for Jelle Vanendert for "one last time". When I arrived, even though I had no right to be there since I had no jersey to take, they had let me into the protocol perimeter so that I could approach Jelle. I had tears in my eyes; I was more moved than at the time of my own victories because I knew what that represented for him. Jelle was the unluckiest of people: slipped disc, operations, recalcitrant knees, he had been drooling about it since the beginning of his career. Because when you're with someone for 24 hours a day as we were, you can imagine the complicity that is forged. This victory was delectable; it was perhaps the most moving moment of the Tour for me because I was sharing my friend's happiness. I'm often asked why he won't be coming with me to BMC. Quite simply because he had chosen another option beforehand, but I hope that we'll find each other again. Over the whole of my season, I owe him an enormous amount, and he knows it.'

Jelle Vanendert, unlike Pantani, Armstrong or Contador, was not however to win the Tour in Paris, but that's another story! On that subject, in the evening of the Pyrenees, nobody knew who was going to win the Tour because, curiously, the big names had not taken advantage of the hilly Pyrenees region to attack themselves. It was only partly postponed...

CHAPTER 23
The Big Buckle is Buckled

In Montpellier also, the weather was awful! Incredible, all the same, in that summer that wouldn't get going, all those holiday makers who had exchanged their parasols for umbrellas. It made the café owners and the TV viewers happy: people prefer to watch TV rather than to stand in the rain and the TV ratings were benefiting from it to the full. In Herault, one didn't have to be a soothsayer to know that the hero of the day would once again be Cavendish, who had taken out an option on the green jersey by winning a new stage. The second rest day occurred in Provence, in the truffles region of Saint-Paul-Trois-Châteaux, where the comments were coming thick and fast, like that of Cavendish, when advancing his pawns on the third week's strategy. Who was therefore going to win this Tour? *Cadel Evans was not attacked in the Pyrenees, he was shown to be the most incisive, he has won a stage, he was never trapped and was stronger than his rivals in the stopwatch event. For me, he's the favourite.'*

The Schleck brothers were reproached for not choosing one of themselves as the true potential winner, especially as several competitors had been eliminated, swept away by the falls. And then, on the morning of that last rest day, Thomas Voeckler was still in yellow. He had suffered certainly in the Pyrenees but was still good, with his usual valour, his determination and his recent paternity, which made him even stronger in adversity. In Valency, where the Omega Pharma-Lotto team was resting, Jelle Vanendert had posed with a polka dot jersey that was far too big for him. He had discovered with amazement, in the Press, that the last Belgian winner of a great mountain stage was called Lucien van Impe, in Saint-Lary-Soulan, in 1981. Neither Jelle nor Phil had been born! On that morning, the *L'Equipe* newspaper had taken advantage of it to announce that Phil and Hushovd would be riding together for BMC by 2012.

'I hadn't wanted to go to the press conference on the rest day but I had to, with Jelle. And I had refused to deal with any question relating to my future, as I had previously stated. I couldn't confirm a piece of information that wasn't right at that time since I hadn't signed anything anywhere. We were fully enjoying our successes, with the Omega Pharma-Lotto team, and I found it exasperating to have to suffer once again from the assumptions of the Press, but that was the name of the game, and I had to put up with it.'

'The stage that ran towards Gap was undoubtedly the last that could correspond to my temperament and/or my desires. But like the previous week, I was marked to the seat of my pants. Do I have to explain to them more concretely that the green jersey doesn't interest me for them to leave me in peace? I had the feeling, above all, that Cavendish and company were afraid of the Alps and of failing to make the time limits. So they were still wary of me. I tried however but I received no exit visa. Moreover, it had to be wanted, a breakaway group. The temperature had been mild, the day before, and then suddenly the storm thundered, and it became six degrees colder. At certain places, on the road, there were still some hailstones; it was impressive. One had to get cosy or to leave. And Contador did it. There, he had amazed me because he had used a transition stage to regain some form in relation to the Schlecks. After the Manse pass, in the famous descent which had been fatal to Beloki and which had almost misled Armstrong without the crossing of the wheat field, there were riders everywhere. A colony of elements lost in the rain.'

In front, the Norwegians Hushovd and Boasson Hagen were proving that a country represented by two riders could animate a Tour De France. The Schlecks were also two for Luxemburg but things were going less well for them: Contador had made up his delay on Andy, feeling the cold on the icy and slippery roads, petrified by the fear of a fall. It was a frosty reception: the man from Madrid had regained his strength and Cadel Evans, for his part, without warning, was still there. He had still not made a fault. Making one the next day was disadvised. 'The arrival in Pinerolo in Italy had been particularly detailed and highlighted by the organizers themselves, in other words, they wanted to warn to us at all costs for the final sprint. I admit that at *that particular moment, my heart was no longer really in my work. We were less involved, Jelle couldn't aim for a general jersey, for the polka dot it was complicated, and as I was always marked in the possible breakaway groups, I was finding it hard to motivate myself but I was doing my job by placing Jelle at the foot of the passes. For him, however, there was no longer any surprise effect of the Pyrenees, and the others were wary about him too.'* The descent towards Pinerolo enjoyed, fortunately, some better weather. It wasn't raining in Italy but that didn't prevent some of them from paying a visit to the terrace of a private courtyard. Hivert and especially Voeckler missed a turn at the same place. The Alsatian was to lose thirty seconds in the adventure. Contador, helped by Samuel Sanchez, went on the offensive once again and Boasson Hagen brought a fourth victory to Norway!

The first visit to the Galibier was frightening everyone, the more so as, three days earlier, it had been snowing at the top of the famous pass that was celebrating its centenary in the Tour De France.

"I no longer had had a precise mission except that of defending Jelle's polka dot jersey. At the briefing, the watchword was to keep an eye on Roy and Chavanel who were used to leaving in the breakaway groups and to scoring points. I stuck to Sylvain, who indeed left. The champion of France and the champion of Belgium united, it was lovely, but I couldn't ride. He was finally in my situation when I was neutralised for the green jersey. I had however not ridden against him, I don't like that and he knows it, he's a rider whom I respect, we often took part in final sprints together, I wasn't there to sabotage him. On the Agnel pass, I was surprised to regain a kind of motivation at 2,500 metres of altitude, all the same, I was good but, on the Izoard, after having done my job for Jelle, I opened up a gap and I waited for the gruppetto, which only caught up with me on the Lautaret, the slope that leads to the Galibier. When I saw the guys' heads, all pale, I reckoned that there was a problem. In fact, they had been going hard for a moment for fear of arriving after the deadlines. I had followed calmly, without drawing from my reserves, even though, indeed, we were beyond the deadline but there were so many of us that the regulations required us to be reinstated. On the other hand, a penalty

of twenty points was imposed on those who were playing for the green jersey, which is why I had never understood why Rojas, who was distinctly better in the mountains than Cavendish, had not, on that particular day, used this item of the regulations to detach himself, to arrive within the deadlines and to get back some points.'

Andy Schleck, for his part, had arrived much earlier, helped upstream by a remarkable race of preparation from Maxime Monfort, who had left in the breakaway group before waiting for his leader who had detached himself on the Izoard. The performance of the younger of the brothers from Mondorf was prestigious. An attack from afar in the mountains by a leader: one had had to wait for ages to see that. On the other hand, for Contador, the Tour was finished. What he had shown in the previous stages was only an illusion, powder in the eyes: left behind on the Galibier, he knew that he was not going to win a fourth Tour. Conversely, Cadel Evans, alone at the controls of the pursuit with Voeckler and Roland on his wheel, maintained his chances by climbing the Galibier like a master and by offering the last bit of suspense to Voeckler, heroic in the defence of his tunic.

'The stage towards the Alpe d'Huez was the one that frightened me the most because it was short, 109 kilometres, but terribly difficult with tired bodies. As from the Télégraphe, there were some in every direction, it was impressive, it was a stampede. I had stuck with the main group but as from the Galibier, I had had to come unstuck. Afterwards, we descended the Lautaret against a headwind and I then ascended the Alpe d'Huez with Jelle Vanendert. He was done for as well: he knew that it was finished for the polka dot jersey. We were thinking of one thing only when ticking off the snares of the Alpe: of Paris, with the certainty, barring mishap, of arriving there and concluding, especially for Jelle, to whom I had often said: "When are you giving up?" At the arrival, I heard someone shouting from a VIP bus; it was a supporter friend, Robert Belhomme. With Jelle, we entered the enclosure and we drank two glasses of champagne in seven minutes. My head was spinning straightaway. The altitude, the fatigue, and I had eaten practically nothing all day: you can imagine the context! My hotel room had a terrace, I had a splendid view and I saw the last riders arriving, it was a bit special.'

Samuel Sanchez, fresher, was from now on definitively the winner of the polka dot jersey. The Omega Pharma-Lotto team did not have too many more opportunities for dreaming in this Tour of total suspense: Voeckler had cracked on the new version of the Galibier as a result of the thrusts from Contador and Andy Schleck. Returned in the valley thanks to Pierre Roland, he was to be unable to hold the distance on the Alpe d'Huez where his young teammate and a future white jersey easily dominated the Contador-Sanchez pair. The first French victory for Roland on that Tour also meant the change of yellow jersey for the first time in ten days: it passed from the Voeckler's to Andy Schlecke shoulders, who had had a lead of less than a minute over his brother and Cadel Evans in the previous day's stop-watch event in Grenoble.

'Law-breaking on the way to Grenoble'

'I had a good night but, on the other hand, we had had to get up early in view of the transfer to Grenoble. This was undoubtedly the most stressful part of the Tour. On the descent of the Alpe where the official cars normally have the right to overtake, some stewards had assumed the role of policemen by refusing the passage. It was chaos: they wanted absolutely that the letter of the law be obeyed, which I furthermore considered to be entirely logical, but not on that particular day. There ought to have been priority for the riders required to be present at the start of the stopwatch event! In the valley, the road was blocked too. An ambulance saved the day by taking the left-hand lane with all its sirens blaring. Ahead, the traffic had made way and we had followed right in the ambulance's wake. Very soon, there were many sports managers' cars behind us but, despite everything, it remained stressful. Just imagine how it must have been for those who were playing for the yellow jersey that day! We were law-breakers, and the drivers ahead were spitting blood, but we absolutely had to stay in the ambulance's wake. At a given moment, I saw a police car on the side of the road, and it immediately got on to our tail, with its revolving lights flashing. I told myself that our Tour was finished, that we were off to prison! But when the police car drew level with us, it on the contrary served as an escort for us and

ask us to follow it. I heaved a huge sigh of relief. I arrived stressed but heated by the circumstances! I had prepared suitably, I didn't have a huge amount of strength but I wanted to take this stopwatch event seriously and I was doing some frankly interesting times until the moment when I derailed three times consecutively. My bicycle had been badly adjusted, and once again I had my cyclo-cross reflexes to thank for avoiding a painful fall on my frame. I still wonder how I didn't break anything and I know that many television viewers were hurting for me, but I can reassure them, I had avoided a painful injury (...). On the other hand, I didn't not want ride any more, it was finished, I was unfocused, annoyed. What a bad advertisement for our equipment! I had watched the Andy Schleck-Evans duel on television by inflicting a painful programme on myself where some people invited as so-called cycling specialists recounted no matter what, I no longer know on which channel, but without mincing my words, it was really piss poor. I'm always staggered, during the Tour, by the number of characters who, all of a sudden, are interested in cycling and virtually teach you your trade when you hear them speaking. I had guessed that Cadel Evans was going to impose himself, as his delay on the Schleck brothers was not enormous and, since the beginning, in any case from Mûr-de-Bretagne, I had had the feeling that he was the favourite.'

Like Phil, the Schleck brothers had had to wade through the traffic jams and leave a lot of nervous energy in them, but that took nothing away from the Australian's demonstration, who, contrary to the Luxemburgers, had taken part in that same stopwatch event around Grenoble in the Dauphiné Rally. It was not a detail and it made a clear difference for the man who was fed up with places of honour on the Tour. Evans won the Tour itself and donned the yellow jersey for the first time on the day before the arrival, sharing the podium with the winner of the stage, the new the stopwatch star, Tony Martin.

'A new version of ecology'

'The following day, we had a transfer to Paris by plane. There, it
was a bit of a mystery for me. For three long weeks, the organizers
had been repeating their ecological messages to us by asking us to
jettison our water bottles only when there were spectators around so
that they could recover them, by inviting us to leave our energy bar
wrappers in the dustbins envisaged for that purpose, and yet here
was a Qatar Airways plane coming empty from Doha to take us to
Paris, when we could easily have taken the HST ! In the spirit of
anti-pollution, admit that there could have been a better way. At the
start, I had had the pleasure of seeing Patricia again, whom I had
already greeted at Gap. I was completely relaxed even though we still
had one more mission: to try for the stage victory on the Champs-
Elysées with Greipel. At four laps from the end, Frison had let out
a yell because we were too far behind the peloton with Jelle. He was
really not content, we obeyed, I went up to the front, and in the end,
I did a kilometre at more than 60 kph but Cavendish was really
unbeatable. It was finished, or almost. On the podium, I was invited
to exchange a Province of Liege flag and another from the Vendée
with Thomas Voeckler. That meant the passing of the baton between
the start of 2011 and the start of 2012, and I was pretty proud of that
favour: it meant a lot to me. We then had a drink in the bus as team
mates before the famous procession on the Champs-Elysées. We took
many photographs, also, because we had had, although you wouldn't
think so, a fabulously successful Tour with a collection of jerseys and
three stage victories, which was no mean thing. With a minimum of
success, I had bagged a couple more. On the Sunday evening, in Paris,
like all the others, we had gone out to celebrate but at 3 o'clock in the
morning, I threw myself on my bed in a sorry state: I was, as one says
in today's parlance, "legless". I hadn't forgotten, either, to salute Evans
for his performance: he had deserved it a hundred times over. So the
Tour was well and truly finished.'

CHAPTER 24

A Basque Beret For Me!

When the Tour has been completed, it's commonly said, it's a Monday that follows: what are we going to do with ourselves today? There's nothing on the telly! For the athletes, the heroes of the longest race of the year in its physical and mental approach, it's very different. They start the round of the rallies, a kind of festive prolongation of their sufferings of July, which enables the public to salute them, to thank them and, for the riders, to stuff their wallets.

In the immense Concorde La Fayette Hotel, at the foot of the Porte Maillot Palais des Congrèss in Paris, the alarm clock was painful for certain. *'As soon as I was ready, we took the road with my faithful masseur, Dirk Leenaert, heading for Alost! It was the first rally of my round and I was not surprised by size of the crowd when we arrived. That festive town, famous for its carnival, had amassed 55,000 people, according to the organizers, on a course of 1.8 kilometres. The atmosphere was unique: we really benefited from the public in a different approach than when we are in competition. We were cool and relaxed!'*

'Helped out by Andrea Tafi'

Flanked by Jelle Vanendert who, contrary to other years, came to a rally as a star, Phil made the clapometer explode. *'With a few laps to go, I had a fright however, because I had a puncture. Andrea Tafi, who was taking part in the "veterans" race, was in the vicinity and he immediately helped me out with a rear wheel. I was as proud as Punch and moved because Tafi, for me, is one of the greats of cycling and I'm one of his biggest fans. Inevitably, he shone in the classics, and he had a broad enough range, like me today. He was at the end of a career when I began mine and I had had the honour of riding beside him; I remember it perfectly. I had won the race by detaching myself before the arrival ahead of Samuel Sanchez and Ivan Basso. On the podium, we received enormous glass of a local beer, it was very nice, a really pleasant memory.'*

The entrance fee debate

'*After the race, my parents came to see me in the hotel: I hadn't seen them for more than a month. It's very important for my balance to maintain contact with my family, with my roots, with my unit. On the Tuesday, off to Roulers for our second rally with of course Jelle Vanendert . The scene was remarkable once again but there were fewer people, for a very simple reason: there was an entrance fee. I took advantage of it to open a little debate on the subject because, generally, people get offended when askd for an entrance fee for a cycle race. It is also said: "Cycling, the only free sport in the world". Is it not precisely because it is systematically free that it is suffering, financially? Because let's not kid ourselves, and I had said it once again on the eve of the Tour of Lombardy, our sport is ailing. The crisis is driving the sponsors away, cyclists are finding themselves unemployed, and so on and so forth. I'm an absolute fan of motor rallies: whether the rally is small scale or world level, an entrance fee is always paid. When they go to see a football match on a Sunday morning with their feet in mud on the side of a provincial pitch, people are also asked for money. I am therefore not opposed to a contribution from the public, a fortiori on races where there are circuits. But I'm absolutely against the virtually total privatisation of the strategic places and the finishing lines for erecting marquis there where VIP tickets are sold at prohibitive prices, which excludes many supporters who can't afford them. Because that hints at exploitation.'*

'*In short, in Roulers, even though there were fewer people, the atmosphere was exceptional. Unlike the day before, the race was more complicated. On the last lap, Samuel Sanchez got free. We came out of the peloton with Thor Hushovd to catch him up, but it was too late. I finished second ahead of Thor.*' Happy, Sanchez was to acknowledge his enthusiasm for the exceptional Belgian public and he announced, above all: '*I'm making a date with Philippe, on Saturday, in Saint-Sebastien.*'

'*Thor, precisely, had asked me to accompany him for the rally in his country, Norway. However, it had just been struck by two murderous*

tragedies. The country was in mourning but rather than cancel the
rally, the people in charge had decided to maintain it in to bring a
few smiles and some recreation to the public, terrorized by the events.
Butchery like that in a country of 4.5 million people marks the minds.
Thor had been affected by it. He had been surprised by the violence
of the event, telling me that, in his country, there were never any
brawls or conflicts. We had offered people a little pleasure: it had
been compelling. We were 65 riders at the start, some twenty of whom
were Belgians, and the level was pretty high. The principle was very
different from in Belgium where we take part in races of 80 to 100 km,
but up there, on a very technical and undulating course of 1.4 km, we
initially raced for an hour and then there were five laps at the end. I
had no experience of that system, and I had to adapt to it because the
placement was important. I had furthermore been taken by surprise
at the start and had lost some places. I had had to wait until the last
six laps before getting to the head of the peloton and being able to
attack immediately and, get just ahead of Cancellara!'

'In the evening, we had celebrated our successes on the Tour a little
with Thor and I had got to know some local stars, world and Olympic
champions in skiing and other Scandinavian sports. I admit that I've
forgotten their names but meeting them was very enriching.'

'The next day, I was back in Belgium to take part in another rally,
in Herentals, the stronghold of Rik van Looy, whose record the
specialists were claiming that I could equal. What pride if it could
turn out to be true! There again, the public was very present and
overheated, as in Alost. Van Looy is a legend, like Eddy Merckx, and
I feel humbler compared to them. Insatiable, I came back on Nibali
and Basso who had left as a tandem in a breakaway group, I caught
up with them and then passed them to finish on my own ahead of
Nibali a few seconds later, and Leukemans, who had managed to
overtake Basso.' 'That night, I slept in the house of my friend and
teammate, Adam Blythe, because, on the Friday, I was taking part
in my fifth and final rally, that of Saint-Nicolas. The crowd there was
huge once again, the course was fast and, fortunately for us, for the

public and for the organizers, it wasn't raining because the paving stones, smooth and shiny, could have constituted permanent dangers.'

In Saint-Nicolas, there is a tradition which the organizers try to respect: to have, at the start, the winner of the Tour. Cadel Evans had not only agreed to be present but, at the red flame, he took to his heels and in spite of Phil's sprint, he won all on his own, with McEwen coming to take third place. *'We had a good laugh with Cadel: he had a yellow jersey that was three sizes too big for him! He was also fresher than I in the race.'*

To the Basque Country by Private Jet

'When the rally had ended, we were rushed to the airport under police escort where, supreme luxury, a private jet was waiting for us to take us to the Basque Country. That had been a part of the conditions in order to enable us to take part in the Saint-Nicolas rally. A cyclist who was coming from the Netherlands arrived late and, because of him, we had been unable to land on the Saint-Sebastien Airport's runway because it had closed at midnight! The plane put down on another runway, some 100 kilometres away. One of the team's trainers came to find us. Although he had done the journey twice, he managed to get lost, thus delaying things still further until we got to bed at around half past two in the morning. I hadn't even had time to have a shower since the rally! And all we had had to eat was three little ham rolls! So you can imagine that state I was in when I got the start of the Saint-Sebastien Clasica a few hours later! We had furthermore gone to the start by bike, it was less risky, but I had the feeling of no longer knowing where I was, I was tired, and my head was heavy. I had dozens of request for photographs and I acquiesced, without asking any questions of that enthusiastic Basque public.'

In the hunt for points for recovering the place of world number one that Cadel Evans had snatched from him at the conclusion of the Tour, Phil had never won the Clasica, a classic that suited however his punchy temperament. During the rallies, Samuel Sanchez had repeated: *'Only a rider who* can stay with Philippe will have a slight chance of winning.' The Asturian's predictions came terribly true. Among the 19 victories of the season, this one, despite the admittedly reduced media coverage, was worth its weight as an athletic feat.

'Despite the tiredness, the complicated journey and the hours of sleep that could be counted on the fingers of one hand, I was good right from the first turns of the pedals. We had placed Klaas Lodewyck in the breakaway group and that had directly put us in a strong position. Once again, the entire team was on top form. Several times, during the race, I had said to Jelle that I was going to win and I don't know, each time, he had burst out laughing as if I had said something silly to him. Because we had been unable to talk to each other via the earpiece: the person in charge of the communication system had quite simply forgotten to bring the equipment. As if a football dressing room attendant had forgotten the guys' boots. Negligence that we frankly considered unforgivable because, beyond the potential victory in the Basque Country, Omega Pharma-Lotto was also playing at the table of the first team place in the world. So we operated as in the good old days, by feeling, and it all went down very well. The more we advanced, the better I felt. Before the last ascent of the Jaizkibel, I had once again repeated to Jelle that I was going to win and he had laughed out loud, but not without famously skimming the competition. He had offered me an ideal launching pad and at the approach of the last hill, I left at three kilometres from the arrival and nobody saw me again. I hadn't thought that I would win that classic, frankly, but I was very strong because I had accomplished the last two kilometres as though in an against-the-clock event with my hands on top of the handlebar without losing a second on those who were pursuing me.' Including some Belgians, Van Avermaet and Devenyns in particular, who had also put on a good show, that day. On the podium, Phil received the famous Basque beret with its impressive diameter. 'Thor Hushovd had sent me a message in English of course ("Congratulations for the stage victory at the 27th stage of the Tour De France ") because it was true that I had just pulled off a feat by wearing a number on my back for 27 days *running, even though there had been two rest days during the Tour!'*

On the subject of the number, Phil had inherited the famous 51, in Saint-Sebastien, the number immortalised by Eddy Merckx in the 1969 Tour, and which, ever since, has preserved its legendary aspect in the peloton.

'I was happy because all at once I had bagged 80 points for World Tour and had added a prestigious victory to my 2011 record! I was now 92 points behind Cadel Evans: it was really an excellent operation. Fortunately, we spent the night in Spain because I would have had neither the courage nor the strength to take the plane on that same evening. That particular Sunday was actually my first day of rest. Because on the Monday, I was committed to the rally of Lommel, in Jelle's stronghold. I would have liked to have seen Jelle win, but the Limburg-oriented competition, of which I was unaware, played in my favour. We were initially in a breakaway group before the fall of an advertising banner that was promoting the grouping. But I set out again afterwards to finish on my own ahead of Fränk Schleck and Jelle Vanendert. I was then in a hurry for only one thing: to go home. On the Tuesday, I was at home, exhausted, but so happy to see my loved ones.'

CHAPTER 25

Champion of Belgium Once Again!

In Monaco, Phil immediately resumed his habits: training with his friends, and fitness sessions.

'I added, however, some exercises on my stopwatch bicycle because I was preparing for the Eneco Tour and I imperatively to work on my against-the-clock if I wanted to achieve something of value in that event. Forced labour after the Tour? Not, it was an interesting possibility for collecting points for the World Tour and then the Eneco is a race that really suits me, that I am certain to be able to finish among the first five because it allows me to use all my assets: to go quickly in a short stopwatch event, to be able to rub in a final sprint or in an advantage and to survive a stage in the Ardennes, is exactly the context of the Tour of Belgium or the Ster Electro Tour but with two days of racing moreover. I had therefore also multiplied the stretching sessions, in the gym, to put my body "right" after the accumulation of journeys from one rally to another, of exhausting trips to Norway and then to Spain.'

Meanwhile, there was consternation in cycling circles, or at least a surprise that was nevertheless not unexpected: Omega Pharma announced the sponsor with which it would be working during the next season, Quick Step! However, Phil had never concealed his contacts with Quick Step, contacts with Patrick Lefevere that had been going on for several months. All that to find himself with the Omega Pharma leaders again, with whom he had had some tense and tricky relations, to say the least. Cornered by the Press that was asking him for his opinion, Phil lashed out in a communiqué that he sent to the "Soir.be" website, because he had other things to do while in full preparation for the Eneco. *'I regret discovering through the Press that Omega Pharma has associated itself with Quick Step, I would have preferred, out of respect for my results and the knock-on effects that I bring to my sponsors, to have been informed of it by them themselves. For recall, I am the only one to decide what my next sporting plans will be. To date, Lotto, BMC, Quick Step and Astana have all made me a sportive and financial proposal, all of which are of interest. The Tour De France has comforted me in my choice. I regret being unable as promised to inform my loyal supporters and the Press about my decision, but please know that that will happen at the appropriate time. One last thing: I will fight until the end of the season for the colours that I'm wearing this year, and also and especially for my fantastic team mates.'*

Phil kept his word to the letter by approaching the Eneco with enthusiasm, as did his entire team. The former Tour of the Benelux Countries began on 08 August with a prologue of 5.7 km in Amersfoort, in the Netherlands. It was dominated by the young American prodigy, Taylor Phinney, who was still unaware, at that moment, that Philippe Gilbert was to be his team-mate at BMC. Troubled by health problems at the beginning of season, the former student of Axel Merckx at Livestrong won his first professional victory at the end of a superb demonstration in front of other specialists, including, not the least, the likes of Boasson Hagen and David Millar. *'Which is why my eighth place, in that context, was a fantastic result. I had asked the team to have Michiel Elijzen as sports manager in order to perfect our automatic steering mechanisms for the stopwatch events. However, there were two of them in the Eneco before the third, very important for me, that of the championship of Belgium at Tervuren. If I'm talking about that, it is because the sports manager, in the car, is like a real navigator in an against-the-clock, exactly like the person who reads the maps in a car rally.'*

At the end of the first stage, it was already party-time at Omega Pharma-Lotto, since Andre Greipel had won it at the sprint ahead of Galimzyanov, the young Russian who had been winning regular runner-up places since the beginning of the season. *'The guys got through a fantastic amount of work: Debusschere was in the breakaway group, Philippe had prevented my being surrounded by the Rabobanks and Sieberg did the rest to take me along to the sprint,'* explained the German, chilled to the bone by a winter wind in Saint-Willebrord. On that same day, an important piece of information was communicated by the BMC team: the American formation had just signed Thor Hushovd for three years. This transfer was represented, for the majority, as the aperitif before announcing the arrival of Philippe a few days later, but Phil was keeping mum on the subject.

'Yet another victory in Wallonia'

The next day, the peloton arrived in Belgium in Ardooie, and under the same conditions, wind and rain, Greipel gave Farrar and Boasson Hagen a hiding after having been brilliantly taken along by Roelandts. The 'Gorilla', as he had been nicknamed, was on magnificent form. The team too. That fell even better as the Queen Stage was on the programme with the course between Heers and Andenne via the famous Wall of Huy, far too far away from the arrival, however, to constitute a decider.

'Roelandts and Vanendert once again did an exemplary job at the end. Because Boasson Hagen was lying in wait, he was improving, and I really felt that the Norwegian was up for it. On the Ben Ahin hill, Jelle set the pace flat out for as long as possible then I left at seven kilometres from the arrival, despite the headwind. It wasn't easy; I wasn't feeling above the fray like on other occasions. I had kept a slight lead on the dip but I knew that if I could keep a lead of even 100 metres before the last little bump at two kilometres from the arrival, it would be OK. There again, I devoted myself as in a stopwatch event, I was getting ready for the exercise of the following day to some extent, and it was very interesting. I had located the arrival at the time of the first passage, a particularity that I encourage furthermore, in relation to the organizers, because it is always interesting for us to discover the pitfalls once it has become impossible to reccy all the races. I sprinted flat out, even though I already had a little lead, because I wanted to make a as big a gap as possible in relation to the stopwatch. It was a great victory, yet another one in Wallonia, moreover, after those of Eupen and La Gileppe, there was a lovely atmosphere and, of course, my supporters. I had taken the leader's jersey from Boasson Hagen with a lead of five seconds, but I knew that it wouldn't be enough.'

'To wear the tricolour jersey in Liege in 2011'

In fact, in the Roermond against-the-clock, another young prodigy and another former pupil of Axel Merckx, Jesse Sergent (New Zealand) dominated the stopwatch event thanks, admittedly, to the changing weather conditions (he had started when it was dry). Boasson was 9th, Phil 25th. '*It was however a good performance overall because I finished second in the final ranking behind Boasson Hagen but in front of some pure stopwatch specialists such as Millar, who had had an ideal terrain for expressing themselves. I could have taken advantage the last stage which contained some pitfalls but the wind was against us in the Visé region, and nobody could avoid the massive sprint won by the winner of the final classification, which made his success even sweeter. Second on a podium between Boasson Hagen and David Millar, at in mid-August, three weeks after the Tour, that had its appeal all the same. The more so as with the six points for my stage victory and the eighty allocated for my second place, I was getting closer to the classification of the World Tour. I was now only a whisker away from Cadel Evans. I could already have bagged first place in the Eneco Tour but, finally, it was better like that: I was obliged to remain focused on my future missions.*'

The next one was the strangest of the season. Because several months previously, Philippe had decided to register for the national stopwatch championships. On 15 August, in Tervuren, the weather was gloriously set fair and the organizers, a little anxious about the date right in the middle of the holiday period and especially about that bank holiday that was prolonging the weekend, were wondering how they were going to attract the spectators to their cute little commune. '*But we were quickly gratified, even straightforwardly surprised*', Burgomaster Bruno Eulaerts admitted, Tervuren being completely colonised by the hordes of Philippe Gilbert's supporters coming from Remouchamps and elsewhere for a good day out.

'Michiel loses my bike !'

'*I had had a good feeling about this stopwatch event, quite simply because I had meticulously prepared for it. Firstly, to have taken part in the Eneco was not a detail since it comprised two against-the-clock events. Then, I had insisted on having Michiel Elijzen. The Dutchman was a former against-the-clock specialist. I had furthermore gone to Tervuren directly on the evening of the Eneco*

Tour in order to stay in the area with Dirk and Michiel. Like that,
I could benefit from an evening massage and get some rest. On
15 August, in the morning, I had gone on to the course and after half
a lap, I had met Maxime Monfort. We continued together, and I
tested myself on the bends, which were numerous. I did a lap flat out,
to see, and I realised that I was gaining a lot of speed when the bends
were steep. I was feeling really excellent. In the car, we had had to
do some twenty kilometres to go to a start that was three kilometres
from the hotel because we had slept in an establishment located in the
perimeter of the obligatory point of passage. It was a detail but the
police had in no way wanted to understand, despite our equipment.
That can quickly be irritating. In situ, we had neglected no detail,
installing a motorhome at 400 metres from the start. Then, I had
gone to get my number myself, something which the professionals no
longer do. It suddenly reminded me of my salad days: it was moving.
At the warm-up, I was feeling superb. And in the race, a splendid
navigator because Michiel had noted everything, I could have ridden
with my eyes closed, which, however, would have been dangerous on
such a course. As an aside, and he hadn't said anything to me while I
was riding, Michiel had lost my spare bicycle, which had got detached
from the roof of the car while passing over a speed bump ! He had
continued to speak to me as if nothing had happened. What if I had
had a puncture? I knew the gaps, I had ten then three seconds of delay
behind the best time of Ben Hermans but I knew that I could make
up all that on the portions that suited me. Everyone was wondering
why I was so motivated by this stopwatch event. In order to have both
jerseys in the same season and, especially, to be able to get to the start
of the prologue of the 2012 Tour in Liege dressed as the Champion of
Belgium. I know that it was a question of a long-term vision but it
was from that that I was drawing my motivation. Unfortunately, I
hadn't had time to train after the arrival nor to benefit from it with
the supporters. I had a plane at 19:30 for Nice, Dirk had rushed to
Zaventem whereas I had passed in front of all the youngsters for the
anti-doping control. Always running and rushing, but I was the
Champion of Belgium for the second time in two months !'

CHAPTER 26

In Quebec, I Become Number One Again

More haste, less speed - especially in the event of great fatigue, which was the case not only of Philippe, but also of his 'trainer-masseur-driver-confidant', Dirk Leenaert. When dumping the new against-the-clock champion of Belgium at Zaventem Airport, Dirk inadvertently kept the champion's cycling shoes with him. High treason !

'If there's one bit of your equipment that you absolutely cannot exchange with anybody, it's the shoes. They are bespoke: they're not like the shorts, the jacket or the socks, and so on. They are adapted to your chosen stirrup wedges on your bicycle. I hadn't realised that I had left them in Belgium. It was at the moment of descending for the appointment that I had initially fixed for my cycle-fan friends that I realised that I didn't have them. I apologised to Patricia whom I had bollocked when I got home about what she had done with my shoes whereas she was in no way responsible, and to Dirk Leenaert to whom I had given an earful on the phone. I had found a pair, I had adjusted the wedges and I had left for training ten minutes behind the envisaged timetable. I also like those shoes because they have orthopaedic soles that are inevitably adapted to my feet. In certain formations, you are obliged to choose the team's brand, in others, as was the case at Omega Pharma-Lotto, you can sign a personal contract with a manufacturer. And there, you meet specialists, real professionals who offer you high-performance equipment that is adapted to your needs, it's very important. There is a feeling, also, that develops between you, your feet and the person who is proposing the equipment. In any event, without them, I'm lost !'

'I had been able to add to Alan's wardrobe, who now finds himself with a new champion of Belgium jersey. With the team, I had decided to cancel my participation in the Hamburg classic. I certainly still needed some points for overtaking Cadel Evans but there were other races, no panic, and then I was too tired,

I really had to recover. I was calmly training with my friends when the heat, nearly a heatwave, settled on the Riviera. For the first three days after the championships of Tervuren, I was content with two hours in the morning, and then I pushed more seriously, to four or even five hours, in order to keep an interesting level before leaving for the Plouay Grand Prix.'

'I choose BMC'

Meanwhile, on 19 August at around 9 o'clock in the morning, the American BMC team's website announced that Phil had signed for three years.

'I hadn't been in a hurry to communicate about it but I was pleased that the team had taken care of it. It was a relief because nothing had been settled, and indeed I had had a possible choice elsewhere, at Quick Step in fact. I will not return to the subject in this book, I've spoken enough about it in the Press, but I have respected everyone and all the offers, and I make a point of repeating that. On the telephone, I settled the final details with Jim Ochowicz. I felt a great deal of motivation on the part of the BMC manager, and a great deal of professionalism, too. I was happy with my choice. I had informed my family first, before the official statement came out in the Press, otherwise, except for Patricia, nobody was in the know. Neither my parents nor my brothers had influenced me in my choice. I had chosen all alone in all conscience. What reassured me was the entirely positive general perception of that option. I had heard nobody criticise my decision, only some concerns of the kind: "With Evans and Hushovd, doesn't that make too many leaders?" Public opinion had been also favourable, as I had been able read on the forums. This signing had liberated me, and I had needed it, because at a certain moment, at the peak of the various negotiations and pressures, I had been on the verge of blowing a fuse. I had succeeded in continuing to do my business in circumstances that had not always been simple. To know that everything was settled had enabled me to continue the last part of my season with but a single objective: that of regaining the place of world number one.'

In Plouay, on a circuit that however suited his qualities, and his temperament, in front of a Breton public conquered by his performances and by his knowledge of cycling, Phil was not 'in it', an expression that is not only used in sport.

> 'In my mind, something was missing. What, I didn't know, but it was obvious that the competition was riding against me, I was being marked like never before and I think that that had irritated me. I could say that I abdicated, on that particular day, I postponed even longer the conquest of the few points that I needed to seize the status of world number one from my future teammate, Cadel Evans.'

> 'On 04 September, I set myself another priority: that of taking part in the Bavikhove Rally. The first time that I went there, wearing the Française des Jeux jersey in 2005, I had been treated with great consideration, and nothing has ever changed, even when I became a better-known champion. That's what I like about those organizers, and the reason why they have already been able, for example, to welcome Alberto Contador in person. A relationship of trust has been forged and I've noticed, finally, that I'm pretty loyal to the people whom I like and in whom I have total confidence, which is clearly reciprocated.'

'My escape to Canada'

Although, in previous years, Phil had chosen Vuelta for his preparations for the world championships, his objectives were different this time. The route of world championships of Copenhagen was not what he would have preferred, the Tour of Spain was rather selective, he had left the Tour De France and there were many other opportunities for taking points for the world classification. The Eneco, it was done, Hamburg, he wasn't there and Plouay had been a failure, but it was an opportunity for discovering two one-day races that have been created with resounding success in the Province of Quebec in the previous year. Voeckler had won the Grand Prix of Quebec, and Gesink that of Montreal. The popular and sportive success had been guaranteed.

'I had, indeed, heard good things about it, it was an opportunity for discovering a continent that I knew only by my participation in the world championships of Hamilton in 2003, the first time that I was in the selection as a professional. There were above all eighty points to be taken in each of the two races, which was enormous in view of the tiny number of points that I needed. This voyage had been planned for long time, it was therefore not impromptu. I had furthermore chosen it, in the spring, to give pleasure to my parents by inviting them to accompany me across the Atlantic. It was the first time that they had left Europe. Initially, Patricia was to accompany me but we had been unable to find anyone to look after Alan. I'm not certain, either, that she would have been able to be separated from her infant for one whole week! I had invited my niece and goddaughter Laura, the eldest daughter of my brother Christian, to replace her, and she of course had been delighted.'

In Canada, the organizers don't do things by half. All the cyclists from the Old Continent were gathered at Paris Charles de Gaulle, Terminal 3, heading for Quebec. A flight that doesn't actually exist but cyclists and their entourage are not refused anything. There were a few places available in 'first' and when the team's managers were asked whom they would indicate to sit in comfort close to the cockpit, the sports managers had indicated themselves, by the way. On their arrival in Quebec, in the old city, the cyclists' eyes were open wide: they stayed in Frontenac Castle, that famous residence that dominates the St. Lawrence by its size and its height. To add to the legend of that temple, the organizer, Serge Arsenault, had received his guests in the 'Roosevelt Suite', the very one in which the President of the United States had prepared the various plans for the Normandy landing in 1944. What history!

'Like at the Walloon Arrow'

Phil was received like a prince, welcomed by the local Press with respect and enthusiasm.

*'The motivation that I had lost in Plouay, somewhat regained in
Bavikhove, I had completely recovered over there, for various reasons:
I was far from Europe, I no longer had any pressure, I was popular,
cherished, and superbly accommodated. Then I discovered the circuit
of Quebec. Afterwards, I looked at the weather forecast because when
wet, the course would have presented enormous pitfalls, but when dry
it was splendid.'*

Even deprived of Vanendert, of Van den Broeck inevitably present on the
Vuelta or of Blythe, Phil found his old self again in a climate that he liked.
It was almost like finding himself on the ascent of the Wall of Huy again,
except that the road was wider, but the spectators were enthusiastic and
screamed the name of Philippe Gilbert as though he had always been one of
theirs.

*'I cannot compare this victory with any of the previous ones, this
season, because I quickly found myself on my own for assuming my
responsibilities. Without calling into question, far from it, the quality
of my team mates, I was on my own at the head of a fairly weak
formation. Usually, I always had one or two team mates at the end,
or in the last five kilometres. Here, I had had to speculate on the work
of the other formations, of the other favourites and to avoid taking on
such a workload as, for example, Ryder Hesjedal had done, who had
lost the race because he was riding at the head of the peloton without
a teammate.'*

Tactically, it was a masterpiece. With phenomenal lucidity, Phil could only
adore the pace sustained at the beginning of the race. The Skys of Boasson
Hagen and Gerrans had taken the head of the peloton behind the breakaway
group. *'It was going at 60kph on the flat portions along the St. Lawrence river.
For the first time in such a situation, I felt some stress because I could no longer
see my team mates, and what helped me was the Rabobanks' attack at 70 km
from the arrival. They had exploded the peloton and that had eliminated some
of the adversaries.'*

Compared to the previous year, the organizers had also added an additional bend (an initiative of Charly Mottet, the man who had mapped out the circuit). That had made it possible to eliminate Samuel Sanchez then, especially, Boasson Hagen, who was almost at a standstill. On the approach to the arrival of the penultimate lap, Phil cut the feet from beneath the rest of the favourites by going for his guns already. Crossing the line in the lead at the bell, he was followed by a dozen or so competitors who were some fifteen seconds behind him.

> *'I had preferred to be caught, it was wiser, rather than doing the last lap on my own with the risk of myself exploding on the last bend.'*

Where surrounded by Leukemans, Marcato, Leipheimer, Ciolek and another Gesink, no surprise was forthcoming. At three kilometres from the goal, he made a dart and the end was of a rare intensity. Indeed, only Gesink clung to his wheel, at a good distance however.

> *'I frequently turned around, I saw that he was approaching, I recovered then I accelerated: it was all very intense indeed. And then when I was sure, during the last hundred metres, I let up to enjoy the moment, because I had liked that in the Walloon Arrow! Quebec will remain for me, in 2011, the place where I regained the place of world number one. The place, better, where I had definitively acquired that status. I had met some really authentic people, starting with the organizer, Serge Arsenault, a man of rare humanity, cultured, philosophical, endearing, and almost timeless.'*

A place where Philippe had been able, also, to live from day to day with his parents. After having crossed the line in Quebec and entered the enclosure of the protocol, he embraced Jeannot, Anita and Laura, who had been unable to retain her tears. As for Jeannot, his father, he had uttered these words, stamped with extraordinary emotion: *'Ever since my son has been a cyclist and has been winning races, this was the first time that he has kissed me after crossing the line. I will remember it for the rest of my life!'*

The accommodation, the welcome, the organisation: everything was really perfect. *'On the Saturday, we made the transfer between Quebec and Montreal by train. When I arrived at Montreal, I was welcomed by Louis, a friend whom I had met in Guadeloupe, who showed us the way. I also made another acquaintance, a Swiss, Thomas, who works over there for an international bank. An advantage of the cellphone is being able to find each other quickly!'*

It was also true that, for a few days, Phil had been on the front page of the 'Quebec Sun' and other English- or French-speaking newspapers. *'We went off to ride, as soon as we arrived, after having had a bite to eat at the hotel and, thanks to Thomas, I was lucky enough to discover some splendid places of Montreal, including the Lachine Canal that separates the Old Port from Lake Saint-Louis. Breathtakingly beautiful.'*

CHAPTER 27

From Montreal to Copenhagen

In Montreal, at the top of the hill where Eddy Merckx had won the world championship in 1974, the parks are used for people's Sunday walks. The Indian summer was no myth; the weather was splendid for welcoming the same peloton as in Quebec. On the signing podium, in the wings, the organizers had prepared some panels that they had asked Philippe to sign: *'Gilbert, World Number One, here in Quebec.'* The race, harder, was less animated than the previous one.

'My only fall of the season'

'It was also the only time of the year when I fell! It was after a bend, on a long dip, Dominique Rollin, the Canadian of FDJeux was in front of me, he was holding his handlebar with only one hand while having a drink from other. He hadn't seen the hole in the road and he had a severe fall. I was half a yard behind him, and I couldn't avoid falling. My right hand was hurt very badly, and I took a while before deciding to resume the race. And I then trained for many long weeks with my hand hurting. I was struck, above all by the enthusiasm of the public, once again, which seemed to have known me since time immemorial. That public encouraged me; it had helped me to win in Quebec, and to mount the podium in Montreal. I had asked the organizer for the microphone in order to thank the people: that was the least of things. I hadn't at all thought of doing so beforehand: it came from the bottom of the heart because I had discovered that cycling was not only popular in Belgium or Europe. Sincerely, I had been charmed by the two races, the public, the organizers, it was a splendid memory and I can't wait to return, which will undoubtedly be complicated in 2012 because I'm likely to be taking part in the Vuelta. I hadn't thought that I'd be so well known on the other side of the Atlantic.'

Winner in Quebec, third in Montreal after impressively winning the sprint of the peloton which had delayed (for two seconds) reacting behind the leaders (victory of Rui Da Costa, the Portuguese from the Movistar team who had imposed himself on the stage of the Tour at Super Besse), Phil had, admittedly, done everything to charm the local public. By attacking, by making his mark on the two events, while behaving as the best cyclist in the world, he had offered two lessons of elitism on the classics, which the public knows less well than the Tour De France, which it watches on TV despite the time shift. *'What we miss here, is seeing the great classics live and long',* the organizer, Serge Arsenault explained. *'Which is why what Philippe has shown us here is a priceless.'*

'Jerome D'Ambrosio's wall'

'My only disappointment, finally, was that I didn't receive a jersey for my place of number one. The best rider in the world was perfectly anonymous in the peloton. I know that there's a project to promote that but it's like in politics, it's a project. It has to be validated, studied, and voted. I have however excellent relations with the International Cyclist Union, but this subject is obviously not a priority.'

'When I returned to the hotel after the Montreal Grand Prix, I had handed in my bicycle like everyone else because, to make the flight home, the equipment had to be delivered well in advance. But I had wanted to ride on the Monday for a good clean-up. However, Thomas, my new Swiss banker friend, rode on a Canyon like me. He told me to take my shoes and my pedals and to come to get his bicycle from his office. It was thus that I entered a large international bank of Montreal in cycling gear, in champion of Belgium gear to be precise, and emerged from it with a bicycle! I did the circuit of the Montreal GP again. It's impressive when there are no more spectators, and no more barriers: nothing anymore is recognisable. Then I had met a cycling fan whom I had invited on an excursion, asking him whether he could take me to the F1 "Gilles Villeneuve" circuit. The guy was enchanted and I did a few laps there. I very quickly found the wall

that Jerome D'Ambrosio had crashed into. I took a photograph of it and I immediately sent it to him without giving any details or references. Two minutes later, he answered me: he had immediately recognised the place. Which shows that great drivers have a hell of a visual memory, this in a wink with another world-class Belgian sportsman before whom I bow very low.'

'The Reception in the Lambermont'

'On the Tuesday, I was therefore back in Paris, with jetlag of course and, on my arrival, I left my parents and my goddaughter Laura because I immediately had to dash to Brussels. Vincent was waiting for me in his car and we arrived ten minutes late at a reception at the Lambermont organized by the Prime Minister, Yves Leterme, which had been planned for a long time. He had chosen to receive and honour some sportsmen and women before bowing out of Belgian politics to go to the OECD. I had appreciated his gesture, because it wasn't necessary, I found it really nice, an elegant recognition of the performances of the Belgian sportsmen and women. I had mentioned Jerome D'Ambrosio and then, on the very next day, I found Kevin and Jonathan Borlée again, incredible, no? Then, I dashed to Liege, to the team's hotel. To tell you that I didn't hang around at the Prime Minister's reception, and that I was in Liege before my team mates had returned from Canada ! I had waited for them to be back and then we went out on our bikes, which was essential on the eve of the Grand Prix of Wallonia that was starting from Chaudfontaine. I had taken the others along on the Saint-Nicolas hill, I had wanted to see it again a few months after the Liege-Bastogne-Liege: I couldn't prevent myself. We then returned to the hotel by the roads that I knew by heart.'

'My victory for François'

'I had obviously not been obliged to inflict the Wallonia Grand Prix on myself on returning from my Canadian odyssey but I had *promised it a long time ago to Yves Vanassche, in memory of his son François, about whom I have already spoken: I had come to win, for his memory, for his parents, for his wife and for his children, all so afflicted by that sudden death. On the day of Francois's death, I had furthermore sent a message to Yves in that sense. Now I had to show up and win ! I admit that I had had a strange day, undoubtedly related to my jetlag, with various ups and down. The race was less elevated, given the plateau, but one had nevertheless to prevent a breakaway group from going right to the end. When I saw that everyone was grouped together at the foot of the Citadel, I knew that it was OK. But I wanted to arrive on my own, to have time to salute François and to point my fingers to the sky: I had thought of everything and now I had reached that point. The day before, I had said to Pierre-Yves Hardenne, the ex-husband of Justine Henin, who was on the course, that I would leave on a precise bend, and that is what I did. The following day, after the arrival, he said to me: "But you, you're just not normal !"'*

Up there, the emotion was indeed overflowing. The little Arthur, who resembles his father like two peas in a pod, received Philippe's bouquet, flowers that he will never forget. Surrounded by the Press, Phil didn't hang around. Because he wanted to lengthen his course !

'The 200 kilometres of the race were not enough for me from the point of view of the world championships. With Klaas Lodewyck, we went along the banks of the Meuse as far as Givet, which was 50 kilometres moreover, a good chunk. Dirk Leenaert had collected me, once again, and then drove me to Lille where I was entitled to a good massage, and some rest, before going home.'

'An exchange of watches with Florian Sénéchal'

In Belgium, in view Tom Boonen's expected withdrawal from the Belgian selection for Copenhagen, the pressure was once more on Phil's shoulders, who had chosen to train in Monaco, true to his usual practices.

'The selector Carlo Bomans had programmed a collective training with the others in Overijse, on the Wednesday, but I had declined. The ICU had paid my air fares so that I could be in Copenhagen as of the Thursday. I had indeed been selected as the riders' spokesman to speak in front of 370 athletes, mostly junior boys and girls. I had learned that Carlo Bomans had been annoyed, but so what? He hadn't been in Overijse either, but was already in Copenhagen! I had greatly appreciated that meeting with the youngsters. I had to talk to them about my experience, and I spoke as I always do, with sincerity. On seeing them, I thought to myself that, one day or another, one of them whom I was seeing in the crowd would come and beat me! I felt a little old at that moment. I had devoted myself with pleasure to that information assignment, because when I was their age, there had been no such thing. We had relied on our parents, on our trainers. There was no taking in hand. I'm so attentive to cycling's image that I had immediately accepted that invitation, and it was not out of self-interest, far from it. If I had not had the support of my parents, at that age, I would certainly never have been a professional cyclist. Today, many young people do not have any family support, so they have to be encouraged indirectly, but it's not simple. When I had finished my speech, two young Frenchmen had arrived. One of them introduced himself: Florian Sénéchal. I was wearing my yellow Tour De France watch and he, the same, but a blue one. He had the nerve to propose a swap! The idea suddenly came to me: "If you make the top 5 of the junior championship, I'll give it to you". And on the Saturday, he was fourth, while his compatriot was world champion! I don't know whether my intervention had served as emulation but one has to admit that it was a nice little story. A few days later, I had sent him the watch. I had been staggered by his nerve. When I was his age, the world number one was Lance Armstrong. I would never in a month of Sundays have dared to ask him for his watch!'

CHAPTER 28
My Last Duties

Although the world championships of Copenhagen were being talked about throughout the whole wide world, certain cyclists had discovered the Danish capital only on the day of the start, for the procession that led to the Rudersdal circuit in the remote suburbs, in the countryside, in a word, far removed from the bustle of the city. After Tony Martin's triumph in the stopwatch event and the disillusion of the Belgians in that same exercise, the national team was banking on gold for Philippe Gilbert.

'But I was undoubtedly the only one to believe what I had always said, well before the race, as of the reccy: I was not the favourite: the circuit didn't suit me. Many had believed that it was a stratagem to pile the pressure on to the others, but that was absolutely wrong. That is why I repeated to my compatriots that each of them had a chance, at least those who felt capable. It wasn't a bluff: I was feeling no ascendancy in relation to that circuit: it didn't inspire me - it was as simple as that. But everything was possible. We had a solid selection: with Nuyens and Vansummeren, for example, we had won practically all the classics! But we didn't have a pure sprinter, like Boonen had been. In a race like that one, in good weather, without the slightest wind, that was clearly a handicap. We had no obligation to take the race in hand, no stress. Belgium had done all that it could with the means at its disposal. The course, frankly, was unworthy of a world championship, if the Danes will forgive me for saying so. Fortunately for the organizers, it was Cavendish who had imposed himself. That rainbow jersey, he will often show it since he is the best sprinter in the world but one could just as easily have had an illustrious unknown on the first step of the podium. In relation to my temperament and to the fact that I had often, up to that point, been accustomed to leave, to anticipate, people asked me, after the race, why I hadn't tried anything. It was simple: my speedometer was oscillating for most of

the time between 60 and 65 kph. So to leave on my own at that speed was impossible. Voeckler had tried, at the end, but I think that it was only to get himself seen on television. The British selection didn't make a single mistake; it launched itself from the start with the precise aim of protecting Cavendish, who had ridden for just three seconds in this world championship, the time of his sprint.'

'Belgium, frankly, had done its utmost. I was happy for Klaas Lodewyck, who had been able to take part in the final breakaway group at the end. That meant that he had had the distance in his legs and that his selection was not a subject of debate. When he had been taken, like Olivier Kaisen, the criticisms had immediately gushed forth from all sides. And then? Both cyclists had largely deserved to be in the selection and they had proved it by each taking part in the attacks. I was pleased for that alone, this need to legitimise something. That must be really "Belgian" as a feeling, it is perhaps also for that, among many reasons, that I had chosen a foreign team for the last part of my career. In any case, I had no regrets about having taken Lodewyck with me to BMC: I had urged him to express himself and he had.'

The rainbow jersey was certainly one of Phil's obsessions, one will speak about it again next year, but over there, in the wet of a Danish Sunday dominated by the English, there was absolutely nothing to be done.

'In the evening, I shared a few good moments with my supporters, my family, the ones who had made the trip. I flew back to Nice on the Monday, but I still had some obligations: the Paris-Tours, the Tour of Piedmont, and the Tour of Lombardy. However, unconsciously, I had switched off. When training, I was not focused, and furthermore I didn't ride much, but not a lot was needed to get me up and running again: remember Saint-Sebastien where had I arrived after hardly any sleep.'

In Voves, at the start of the Paris-Tours, in a remote part of the world close to Chartres, Philippe was once again the star of the podium even though

Oscar Freire, with the number one on his back, then leaving Rabobank for Katusha, was applauded as a farewell, and a thank you. Plagued by technical problems, right from the start, Phil looking sombre. Omega Pharma had lined up a team of survivors who had been told a few days earlier that they were already on holiday.

'My sole retirement of the season'

'It was difficult to understand. Finally, not completely: by lining up a good selection for the Tour of Beijing then in Australia for the Herald Sun Tour, the team had received some solid bonuses. I indeed say the team, not the cyclists, and I emphasise that precision. What were its financial needs, on account of a future separation and especially, as of the moment when it was being threatened for the first place in the world ranking? I will never understand that offhandedness. As a result, in the Paris-Turns, nobody was motivated except David Boucher, who had left in the large final breakaway group. When I returned to the bus with David, the others were already showered and changed. They were eating chips and hamburgers and laughingly offered us some. I was furious. I had my shower, I left, I avoided the Press because of the risk of imparting some home truths and I got into Dirk Leenaert's car, heading for Paris-Orly. At 22:30, I was at home in Monaco but, last aside, that was not the right choice. After a long race like a classic, the ideal is to remain on the spot, to get a good massage, to eat and then to sleep, which furthermore is what I usually do.'

'When I found myself at home again, I no longer wanted to leave. But prestige and professionalism generally win the day. I therefore found myself at the start of the Tour of Piedmont, of which I was the double title-holder, surrounded by five team mates! I took that as a total lack of respect. The world number had arrived with a formation that was behaving like amateurs. The race left very quickly, we had Van de Walle in front, I had nothing to hope for from a completely altered course and for the first time of the season, I retired from *the race, at the moment of re-supply, accompanied in particular by Maxime Monfort. I was a little uncomfortable for the public because at the start of the Tour of Piedmont, I had seldom felt such enthusiasm: it was impressive. It's not for nothing that I like Italy.'*

Phil however did not yet disconnect. His pride, and the number one that he was to wear on his back at the Milan start, drove him into forced labour.

'I wanted at all costs to reccy the end of the new course towards Lecco. The others were less motivated but I managed to persuade them: we did a part by car, the rest by bike. The reccy was of paramount importance, firstly because we had to climb the Madonna del Ghisallo by its severest side, then, because the last ascent was interesting. But it was undoubtedly there that I lost any chance of winning the Tour of Lombardy for the third time in a row: at one kilometre from the top of the last difficulty, there was no more signposting. I had asked an Italian touring cyclist who was very nice but who didn't have enough breath to keep up with me to explain the end to me. In fact, I had missed the reccy of the stiffest part of the last bump and the first kilometre of the descent. I had realised my mistake when reading the road book. Too bad: I just had to set out like that. At Omega Pharma-Lotto, they had sent Bart De Clercq to be the seventh man, to make up the numbers. As if to say if the team was fairly worried about the world number one position. However, among the adversaries, it was an obsession. The Sky and the Leopard teams had ridden flat out right from the start, and it had been impossible to follow everyone. Fortunately, the Liquigas had taken things in hand, they had wanted to win with Nibali but for my part, I had very quickly found myself without any teammate. Despite everything, I was feeling good I had seen that Paolini had great ambitions, that Nibali wanted at all costs to win his first victory of the season but when he had started like a madman on the Madonna del Ghisallo, I hadn't responded. At a certain period of the season, I would have been able to respond but there, it would have been suicidal.'

'Out of respect for my team mates'

'I could, also, have left things there but, by principle, even if that team was going to disappear, I didn't want another formation to grab the title of the best team in the world at the conclusion of the last race. I would not have tolerated, having given so much for Omega Pharma-Lotto and having received the support of my team mates throughout the season, that that so coveted, so prestigious element should slip through our fingers. I gave everything at the end, but I came unstuck on the last snares of the hill that I didn't know. When Oliver Zaugg had left, I was convinced that the peloton was going to return and that we would be able contest the sprint but cycling has this original and fabulous aspect that sometimes, fortunately, it offers its champions some unexpected rewards. Monfort, Fulgsang and Zaugg had worked all day long in that Tour of Lombardy. The Swiss was the least known by the public, but not by the riders. I had seen that man on several occasions, in particular when he was at Liquigas, busting a gut for his leaders. A solid climber finally when before the footlights. Omega Pharma-Lotto had saved its number one position. Honour was saved: I would have hated it to have been otherwise. I could leave with a clear conscience, and thank everyone for those three years of collaboration. My season was finished, and what a season ! ...'

MY RECORD IN A FEW FIGURES

Record

Date	Course	Rank
2/6/2011	Palma of Majorca Trophy	157
2/7/2011	Cala Millor Trophy	26
2/8/2011	Inca Trophy	53
2/9/2011	Deia Trophy	86
2/10/2011	Magalluf - Palmanova Trophy	18
2/16/2011	Tour of the Algarve, Stage 1 : Faro - Albufeira	Leader
2/16/2011	Tour of the Algarve, Stage 1 : Faro - Albufeira	1
2/17/2011	Tour of the Algarve, Stage 2 : Lagoa - Lagos	Leader
2/17/2011	Tour of the Algarve, Stage 2 : Lagoa - Lagos	6
2/18/2011	Tour of the Algarve, Stage 3 : Tavira - Malhão	50
2/19/2011	Tour of the Algarve, Stage 4 : Albufeira - Tavira	73
2/20/2011	Tour of the Algarve, Stage 5: Lagao - Portimão	46
2/20/2011	Tour of the Algarve	29
2/26/2011	Het Nieuwsblad	43
3/5/2011	Montepaschi Strade Bianche	1
3/9/2011	Tirreno - Adriatico, Stage 1 : Marina di Carrara C.L.M. (Team)	11
3/10/2011	Tirreno - Adriatico, Stage 2 : Carrara - Indicatore	32
3/11/2011	Tirreno - Adriatico, Stage 3 : Terranuova Bracciolini - Perugia	76
3/12/2011	Tirreno - Adriatico, Stage 4 : Narni - Chieti	10
3/13/2011	Tirreno - Adriatico, Stage 5 : Chieti - Castelraimondo	1
3/14/2011	Tirreno - Adriatico, Stage 6 : Ussita - Macerata	9
3/15/2011	Tirreno - Adriatico, Stage 7 : San Benedetto del Tronto C.L.M.	54
3/15/2011	Tirreno - Adriatico	9
3/19/2011	Milan - San Remo	3
3/27/2011	Ghent - Wevelgem	36
4/3/2011	Tour of Flanders	9
4/13/2011	The Brabant Arrow	1
4/17/2011	Amstel Gold Race	1
4/20/2011	Walloon Arrow	1
4/24/2011	Liege - Bastogne - Liege	1
5/25/2011	Tour of Belgium, Prologue : Buggenhout C.L.M.	2
5/26/2011	Tour of Belgium, Stage 1 : Lochristi - Knokke-Heist	11
5/27/2011	Tour of Belgium, Stage 2 : Knokke-Heist - Ypres	Leader

5/28/2011	Tour of Belgium, Stage 3 : Bertem - Eupen	1
5/28/2011	Tour of Belgium, Stage 3 : Bertem - Eupen	Leader
5/29/2011	Tour of Belgium	1
5/31/2011	Gullegem Koerse	1
6/3/2011	Criterium of Calais	1
6/15/2011	Ster Elektro Tour, Stage 1 : Alblasserdam C.L.M.	17
6/16/2011	Ster Elektro Tour, Stage 2: Eindhoven - Sittard/Geleen	6
6/17/2011	Ster Elektro Tour, Stage 3 : Nuth-Schimmert - Nuth-Schimmert	15
6/18/2011	Ster Elektro Tour, Stage 4 : Verviers (Bel) - La Gileppe/Jalhay (Bel)	Leader
6/18/2011	Ster Elektro Tour, Stage 4 : Verviers (Bel) - La Gileppe/Jalhay (Bel)	1
6/19/2011	Ster Elektro Tour, Stage 5: Etten-Leur - Etten-Leur (Nl)	46
6/19/2011	Ster Elektro Tour	1
6/26/2011	Championship of Belgium S.R.	1
7/2/2011	Tour de France, Stage 1 : Passage du Gois - Les Herbiers/Mont des Alouettes	Leader
7/2/2011	Tour de France, Stage 1 : Passage du Gois - Les Herbiers/Mont des Alouettes	1
7/3/2011	Tour de France, Stage 2 : Les Essarts - Les Essarts C.L.M. (Team)	10
7/4/2011	Tour de France, Stage 3 : Olonne sur Mer - Redon	20
7/5/2011	Tour de France, Stage 4 : Lorient - Mûr-de-Bretagne	5
7/6/2011	Tour de France, Stage 5 : Carhaix - Cap Fréhel	2
7/7/2011	Tour de France, Stage 6 : Dinan - Lisieux	7
7/8/2011	Tour de France, Stage 7 : Le Mans - Châteauroux	14
7/9/2011	Tour de France, Stage 8 : Aigurande - Super-Besse	2
7/10/2011	Tour de France, Stage 9 : Issoire - Saint-Flour	4
7/12/2011	Tour de France, Stage 10 : Aurillac - Carmaux	14
7/13/2011	Tour de France, Stage 11 : Blaye-les-Mines - Lavaur	66
7/14/2011	Tour de France, Stage 12 : Cugnaux - Luz-Ardiden	24
7/15/2011	Tour de France, Stage 13 : Pau - Lourdes	10
7/16/2011	Tour de France, Stage 14 : Saint-Gaudens - Plateau de Beille	68
7/17/2011	Tour de France, Stage 15 : Limoux - Montpellier	28
7/19/2011	Tour de France, Stage 16 : Saint-Paul-Trois-Châteaux - Gap	15
7/20/2011	Tour de France, Stage 17 : Gap - Pinerolo (Italy)	46
7/21/2011	Tour de France, Stage 18 : Pinerolo (Italy) - Col du Galibier	133
7/22/2011	Tour de France, Stage 19 : Modane - Alpe-d'Huez	70
7/24/2011	Tour de France, Stage 21 : Créteil - Paris	87
7/23/2011	Tour de France, Stage 20 : Grenoble - Grenoble C.L.M.	72
7/24/2011	Tour de France	38

Date	Race	Result
7/25/2011	Criterium of Alost	1
7/26/2011	Criterium of Roulers	2
7/28/2011	Criterium of Herentals	1
7/29/2011	Criterium of Saint-Nicolas	2
7/30/2011	San Sebastian Classic - San Sebastian	1
8/1/2011	Criterium of Lommel	1
8/8/2011	Eneco Tour of the Benelux, Prologue : Amersfoort C.L.M.	8
8/9/2011	Eneco Tour of the Benelux, Stage 1 : Oosterhout - Sint-Willebrord	72
8/10/2011	Eneco Tour of the Benelux, Stage 2 : Aalter - Ardooie	66
8/11/2011	Eneco Tour of the Benelux, Stage 3 : Heers - Andenne	Leader
8/11/2011	Eneco Tour of the Benelux, Stage 3 : Heers - Andenne	1
8/12/2011	Eneco Tour of the Benelux, Stage 4 : Roermond - Roermond C.L.M.	25
8/13/2011	Eneco Tour of the Benelux, Stage 5 : Genk - Genk	41
8/14/2011	Eneco Tour of the Benelux, Eneco Tour of the Benelux, Stage 6 : Sittard - Sittard	29
8/14/2011	Eneco Tour of the Benelux	2
8/15/2011	Championship of Belgium (Tervuren) C.L.M.	1
8/28/2011	West France - Plouay GP	57
9/9/2011	Quebec GP	1
9/11/2011	Montreal GP	3
9/14/2011	Wallonia GP	1
9/25/2011	World Championship (Copenhagen) S.R.	17
10/9/2011	Paris - Tours	67
10/15/2011	Tour of Lombardy	8

Some more figures ...

- The number of kilometres covered in races: 12,612
- The number of victories: 24 (including a village fair and five rallies)
- The number of points for the World Tour riders ranking: 718
- The number of points of the Omega-Pharma-Lotto team in the World Tour team ranking (1st team): 1,099
- The number of race days: 84 (including 1 village fair and 9 rallies)
- 1 = withdrawal, fall, and final world tour ranking, charitable work that I support, the Télévie.
- 53 planes over the season
- 34 anti-doping controls

EPILOGUE

Nineteen victories, some among the most prestigious, all the rewards that a cyclist can reap: Philippe has therefore indeed lived a dream year, a year of 'hell', a year of 'phew', as today's cool young things would say. Received in Monaco Palace by the Prince Albert II, to whom he had given his yellow Mont-des-Alouettes jersey, 'Philippe de Remouchamps' was no longer only a Monegasque citizen, but also a recognized world sportsman, which is very rare for a cyclist in the Principality.

The fabulous lap of 2011 had therefore been lapped. It had found its roots in the incredible exploit on the soaked roads of Lombardy. But, except for some filthy weather in Castelraimondo on the Tirreno, the sun had brightly shone on each victory of the World Number One, congratulated and thanked by the president of the International Cyclist Union, Pat McQuaid, on 27 October, the birthday of Phil's son, Alan.

What did Phil have left to dream about? Because it's the dream that motivates the sportsman, far more than the glory or the money. And his mind was full of sporting objectives that required going beyond himself, that so rare faculty that makes the champion. Balanced, blossomed, almost sure of himself, as testified by some of his victories drawn like an architect's plan, Phil has also turned a page: he has changed his team.

BMC will perhaps be his last formation. After having loyally worn the Française des Jeux jersey in his apprenticeship phase, that of Omega Pharma-Lotto in his most prosperous period, here he is facing a new challenge, that of becoming an integral part of a prestigious American team that football fans could compare to FC Barcelona. Rather than bearing the weight of responsibility in a less eclectic unit, Philippe has chosen the difficulty of attracting the services of the likes of Thor Hushovd and Cadel Evans. He has no fear, either, of defying the talented and ambition young lions such as Phinney, Van Avermaet or van Garderen.

His choice had been the subject of debate, because he could have remained in Belgium, but it was dictated by his strict volition to optimise his magnitude, his number one status. The criticisms, nauseating, that emerged at the time of his choice, in August, were inspired only by jealousy because, in the light of what he already brought to Belgian sport, Gilbert deserved, on the contrary, the utmost respect. He knows however that the continuation will be more complicated. He had already measured it in Plouay, in Copenhagen, in the Paris-Tours, and the Tour of Lombardy: when the three colours of the champion of Belgium arrive at the front of the peloton, they become a focal point, a fixation for the adversaries. To keep on winning, Phil would have to be as strong as in 2011, if not stronger.

'To be above all OK in my mind, to have success, and some luck, and to respect my programme. I'll be beaten by some younger riders, so be it, but I'm preparing for it. But meanwhile, other challenges await me: they attract me like a magnet. To win races like the Liege-Bastogne-Liege for a second time, to deny Cavendish at the Olympic Games, to try to land the rainbow jersey, and a Tour of Flanders where I know already the podium, like that of the Milan-San Remo, but not on the highest step. I therefore have a lot on my plate, believe me! I want, also, to please people, to bring them a little happiness. I think of my supporters, of those from the early days, of my family, of all those people who have contributed to my success. They also undoubtedly believe that they have witnessed a dream season and that they will have to wait a while to experience anything like it, but I'm making a date with them in a year's time, right here, in these pages, to draw up the 2012 balance sheet. Perhaps it will be even more glorious? Perhaps it will be less so? No matter what, I will in any event have given my all, as usual, because I'm like that. I've lost races because I had forgotten to calculate, to proportion, to be patient. I've won others thanks precisely to taking a risk. Some call that panache. Me, I call it sport, an exceptional trade that brings me enormous privileges. Yes, I'm well aware of the fact, I'm lucky...'

Phil shares those privileges, returns them as best he can, as soon as he can. Each year, he thus gets involved in the 'Télévie' when his friend Willy Braillard, the former rally and racing driver asks him to, sometimes for a dedicated jersey, sometimes for a presence at a charity evening with the sole aim of raising a little money and bringing a little comfort. Behind the champion, the man has remained what he has always been, brought up to be modest and to respect others within a balanced and tightly-knit family environment. And he has sworn never to forget his basic roots, the ones that had enabled him to become, once upon a time, the World Number One.

CAPTIONS

www.lannoo.com
Register on our website and we will regularly send you a newsletter with information about new books and interesting, exclusive offers.

Author: Philippe Gilbert, in collaboration with Marc Van Staen and Gino Laureyssen
Texts: Stéphane Thirion
Photographs: ImageGlobe (p. 2: Benoit Doppagne, p. 16, 52, 58 and 150: Eric Lalmand, p. 30: Virgilio Rodrigues, p. 36: Luca Bettini, p. 44: Ada Cavaggioni, p. 74: Vincent Jannink, p. 96: Luc Claessen, p. 120 et 128: Peter Deconinck, p. 142: Guillaume Horcajuelo, p. 170: Dirk Waem, p. 186: Bruno Fahy, p. 192: Jacques Boissinot, p. 200: Kristof Van Accom)
Kristof Ramon: p. 10, 22, 66, 104, 112, 206, 216, backcover
Laurent Dubrule: p. 82
Photo frontcover: ImageGlobe/Benoit Doppagne
Translation : Martin Lambert
Concept design: Studio Lannoo

If you have observations or questions, please contact our editorial office: redactielifestyle@lannoo.com

© Lannoo Publishers, Tielt, Belgium, 2011
D/2012/45/180 – NUR 491
ISBN: 978 90 209 1624 9